*What Were Little Girls
and Boys Made Of?*

SUNY SERIES IN EUROPEAN SOCIAL HISTORY

Leo A. Loubère, General Editor

What Were Little Girls and Boys Made Of?

PRIMARY EDUCATION IN RURAL FRANCE, 1830–1880

Laura S. Strumingher

State University of New York
ALBANY

Published by
State University of New York Press, Albany
© *1983 State University of New York*

*For information, address State University of New York
Press, State University Plaza, Albany, N.Y., 12246*

Library of Congress Cataloging in Publication Data
Strumingher, Laura S.
What were little girls and boys made of?

(SUNY series in European social history)
Bibliography: p.
Includes index.
1. Education, Rural—France—History—19th century.
2. Education, Primary—France—History—19th century.
3. Text-books—France—History—19th century.
I. Title. II. Series: SUNY series on European social history.
LC5148.F8S77   372.944   82-3342
ISBN 0-87395-627-3   AACR2
ISBN 0-87395-628-1 (pbk.)

Contents

Illustrations

Acknowledgements

Several individuals on both sides of the Atlantic have been very helpful during the research and writing of this book. Michelle Perrot provided clues to help me track down information at an early stage of my research, while Pierre Caspard and Alain Choppin were most encouraging towards the end. Serge Chassagne opened up the archives at Mont-Saint-Aignan and provided me with pupils' notebooks and good coffee. My old friends in Lyon, the Lequins and Gardens, listened patiently as I recounted the tales from the children's books and tried to make sense of them. Bernard Ben-Soussan and Henriette Pommier shared valuable iconographic sources. Bernard and Corinne DuBlanche, both teachers in Brive, introduced me to colleagues and archivists who rummaged through old books and notebooks to try to help me complete the picture I was so eager to sketch. In Bourges, Jean Jenny helped me locate information about Zulma Carraud. Mssrs. Arcelin and Lanthoinette guided me through the archives at Hachette and found the records pertaining to the sales of Carraud's books.

I am also indebted to many American colleagues who have heard or read large sections of my work on education. Among them I especially want to thank Roger Daniels, Linda Clark, Debra Perry, Carolyn Lougee, Sanford Elwitt, and Patrick Harrigan. I also want to note the hard work of Natalie Roklina and Sheila Lundgren, my assistants with translation on this project, and Barbara Berner, my thoughtful and patient typist.

Finally, I wish to recognize the financial support of SUNY Faculty Fellowship and Grant-In-Aid (Summer 1978), University of Cincinnati Research Council Faculty Fellowship (December 1979), and University of Cincinnati Taft Faculty Fellowship (Summer 1980). Without their support, the research could not have been accomplished.

Introduction

Several years ago, while burrowing in the Municipal Archives of Lyon, I came upon a report by a team of national inspectors about the state of primary school education in that city. The report was dated 1836 and was addressed to the question of how much change had actually taken place since the passage of the Guizot Law three years earlier. The team of investigators reported the lamentable physical condition of most schools, teachers, and pupils. It also commented on the unique arrangement by which the municipal council of Lyon hired various religious orders to teach in all the public schools of Lyon. Finally, the team commented on the books which were being used to teach children the basics — reading, writing, arithmetic, history, and grammar.[1]

It was this last section which really intrigued me. If it were possible to retrieve these books, I believed one could analyze what the children were learning, not only in terms of skills, but more significantly one could pinpoint the underlying values recommended to children in all those books. For the past three years I have hunted for books used by primary schools as readers, since these were the most direct in teaching values. I have discovered scores of books (Appendix A) and many prolific authors: some books which were reprinted dozens of times over several decades, some which had ecclesiastical endorsement, others which were awarded prizes by the state, still others which were translated into English, German, and Spanish. I discovered authors who were former teachers or school inspectors, and some who were social reformers or priests.[2]

The significance of these texts became more and more apparent as I began studying them. The authors of school books for young boys and girls had strong ideas about appropriate social roles for their readers. They helped create not only a literate population, but one which accepted modern ideas.

The school books were vehicles by which authors hoped to shape the future. These writers were members of the middle class, a group which believed in organizing their own lives and futures. This belief was gradually extended to include planning for their sons and daughters and then for the children of the poor. Becoming civilized, a preoccupation of the nineteenth century middle class, meant more education, more polite behavior, more understanding, and helping others to follow suit. Civilization implied a whole social, economic and political program, to be carried out in cooperation with like-minded citizens and inevitably, against those who were labeled obscurantists and reactionary.[3]

French middle-class men and women made themselves the judges of the traditions and beliefs among which they lived. They repudiated dogmas unchecked by reason, the absolute authority of leaders, and the determining influence of the masses.[4] They believed in reason and progress and in their own ability to ascertain what was reasonable and to abet progress. Not surprisingly, they did not always get the cooperation of the people whom they were trying to lead to a civilized life. Peasants, who made up the largest population of those needing progress in the view of the middle class, did not passively accept middle-class ideology. They often worked out their own compromises, evasions, and selections from the portrait of the good life presented to them by middle-class representatives in the primary schools of the nineteenth century.

The primary schools of rural France in the past century are an especially rich source for social historians. First, the readers used in those classrooms were extremely clear in their value presentation (they were writing for children); second, estimates of the number of children affected by this literature can be made from studying publishers' records of sales and from school records of purchases; third, an analysis of pedagogical materials reveals with striking clarity the goals of teachers (many of whom came from rural backgrounds too); fourth, by reading the inspectors' reports we can assess how well teachers were doing in fulfilling the goals of the central authorities. It is far more difficult to ascertain what impact these books actually had on the lives of the pupils who read them. But, by reading memoirs of people who grew up in the countryside, by studying their notebooks which include original compositions, and by studying changes in social roles through an evaluation of trends in marriage and census records, we can begin to get a history of this inarticulate population as well.

Out of the rich variety of data that I gathered in the past three years, I was struck by five main topics, which form the divisions of this book. The poverty of the rural villages and hamlets in the first half of the nineteenth century was the first area of concern. How could areas lacking roads, with scarce populations and little excess wealth obey the Guizot law to establish a school? Next, I was impressed by the pedagogical literature prepared for a new generation of teachers who were to be sent out to work in these poor communities. These teachers were armed with arguments to be made for modernizing. Would their works be well received? I was not surprised to find many examples of resistance on the part of villagers who saw no good reason for their children to learn to read. I was impressed by the rapid growth of religious orders (especially female orders) which were influential in countering parental opposition to schools.

I was particularly impressed by the books of Zulma Carraud, which were directed to socializing rural boys and girls to modern gender roles. Annotated excerpts from her best-selling books, *La Petite Jeanne ou le devoir* and *Maurice ou le travail*, provide a case study of the attempt of the bourgeoisie to inculcate values. These books highlight the growing difference between women's work, which is referred to as "duty" and is portrayed as an expansion of women's nature—e.g., child nurture, house care, care of the sick and elderly, and men's work which remains a duty to his family, country and God, but more importantly becomes a source of fulfillment, provides a sense of achievement and of self-worth. Men use their skills to tame nature, to create civilization, in an ever expanding field of endeavors, while women's work remains tied to a limited sphere. Though in reality woman was not any closer to nature than man, various aspects of her situation (physical, social, psychological) made her appear that way.[5] The view of woman as closer to nature was central to the romanticism of the nineteenth century middle class.[6] Carraud and many other nineteenth century women created institutional forms to embody this belief for their own daughters and for the *filles du peuple* too.[7]

Finally, I was delighted to discover a collection of notebooks kept by children attending primary schools during the nineteenth century. In their compositions one can begin to see the effects of the school socialization process. Similarly, in marriage acts we see a change. Increasingly, during the course of the century, women and men thought it suitable for brides to sign their marriage register, *sans profession,* while grooms identified themselves with many new and diversified jobs. Ironically, the literate daughters and grand-daughters of illiterate women who had registered occupations rang-ing from *cultivatrice* to *propriétaire* were convinced that the best occupation for women was "none." Were they not working? On the contrary, rural women and city women, rich women and poor women, frequently worked as hard as their mates, but their percep-tion of gender role had changed. The work now promoted for women—the nurture of child and husband—was so much a part of the "nature" of woman that it was not viewed as an occupation at all, but as an extension of her being.

PART ONE

Primary Education in the Countryside

CHAPTER ONE

The Poverty of Rural Schools, 1833–1875

In 1833, nearly a century after Condorcet's proposal to educate the people, the Guizot Law was passed requiring every commune (administrative unit similar to a village) in France to provide a primary school for its boys. Free admission was to be given to the poor. Communes were to provide a schoolhouse where the teacher was to live as well as teach, and they were also to pay the teacher a small fixed salary. The bulk of the teacher's income was to come from fees paid by families and, therefore, varied according to the size and the prosperity of the area. Where local resources were insufficient the state promised aid. That was the basic law to which was added in the last article: "Selon les besoins et les ressources des communes et sur le demande des conseils municipaux, il pourra être établi des écoles spéciales des filles" ("Depending on the needs and resources of the communes and upon request of the municipal councils, special schools for girls may be established")[.1]

The Guizot Law reflected a long tradition of valuing boys differently and, in most cases, more highly than girls. A popular saying of unknown origin which persisted throughout the nineteenth century was, "Une fille ce n'est rien, deux c'est assez, trois c'est trop, mais quatre filles et la mère font cinq diables contre le père" ("One daughter is no problem, two is enough, three is too much, but four daughters and one mother makes five devils against the father"). Mothers were known to respond to the question: "How many children do you have?" with the answer, "I have two children and three girls." The resistance to sending girls to school was in most cases stronger than the opposition to schooling for boys.[2]

In practice, what emerged in the middle decades of the nineteenth century was a hodge-podge of public and private schools; most were for boys only, some for girls only, and some mixed. Both religious and secular authorities agreed that the sexes should be separated in school and taught different skills in different manners. Nonetheless, for pecuniary reasons many poorer communes continued to run "mixed" schools through the 1850s.

Even the designations "public" and "private" were misleading. In most cases public instruction referred to a school which was taught by a lay *instituteur* or *institutrice*. But in some cases, like the city of Lyon, municipalities hired teaching orders to take over all teaching responsibilities in schools. Thus, in Lyon, private teachers were those not affiliated with religious teaching orders. In the majority of the communes, however, private teaching referred to religious orders. In any event the commune was not required to have more than one primary school, religious or secular.

Though the material conditions of the schools reflected their environment, some general observations can be made. Religious schools were better funded and better equipped than lay schools; those run by the Brothers of the Christian Doctrine were the best endowed, while girls' schools, funded by the Sisters of Saint Joseph or Sisters of Saint Charles, were a close second. Frequently, the latter institutions ran a two-part school: one for the daughters of the wealthy and one for the daughters of the poor. The money garnered from the first group helped to defray the expenses of the education of the poor, who often resented being kept in a restricted area within the school building.

In the memoirs of a school teacher, Mlle. B. of Gers, written in 1873, we have a poignant recollection of schools segregated according to social background:

In the classroom, no educational material. On the backless benches pushed against the wall, the children quickly became bored. They fidgeted or cried, especially after several blows to the fingers had been administered with a rod.

Our caretaker, a very sick nun, often encouraged us to sleep. "The Blessed Virgin will smile if she hears no noise."

Above our room was a sign, the "Free School." The girls read the Bible, recited prayers, sang hymns, knit, but did not write. Often they were employed at gardening tasks.

In another wing of the convent, the "Paying School" was conducted. This class was comprised of peasant girls and of girls from homes of the urban lower class. They were taught writing. We spoke only to children in our own class.

The same segregation existed in church. On Sunday, relegated to the rear benches, pupils from the "Free School" wore enormous smocks of brown, heavy, rough wool. The hoods were of identical color so that everyone might know that they were charity pupils. I have never forgotten this disdain for the poor.[3]

Religious orders frequently refused to send their members out to work in remote and impoverished areas. The poorest communes thus became the home of the single lay teacher, male or female. On July 12, 1892, Mlle. N., a new teacher in Selles-St-Denis, in the Loir-et-Cher, reported typical conditions in her journal:

Already one month has passed since I have arrived. I have not yet noted anything because I am not yet settled; I think that I will probably never be. How can I settle down? I have no kitchen; or rather the kitchen serves as my classroom; there are children sitting in the fireplace which is sealed up . . . The house belonged to a rich farmer and was never meant to be a school.[4]

It is unlikely that Mlle. N. was exaggerating. The poverty of secular rural schools was generally even worse than that of secular urban schools, whose classes were often held in old buildings constructed for other purposes. For the most part, village schools held classes either in the lower room of a house occupied by the instructor or in a barn or an unused stable. Nor was it rare to see the class held in the instructor's only room, with his bed in the corner. These schools were in striking contrast to the plans drawn up for ideal primary schools as early as 1834[5] (See Illustration 1 and 2).

Instituteurs often had second or third jobs and performed them during class. For example, shoe repair or recaning chairs were common part-time occupations for the poorly paid rural teachers. Simultaneous with the lessons and instructors' other jobs, a *ménagère* would often clean and cook in the same small space. Cows and pigs were not unknown guests in the "classroom." However, this

1. Old village schools

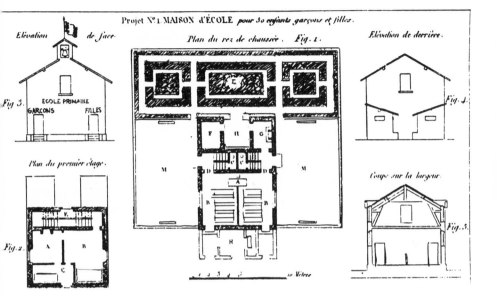

2. Plan for the new school

was not thought of as a problem by most peasant parents who were as yet unaccustomed to separating life from work, or work and family from learning. Book learning gradually became part of the many unconnected and uncritically examined aspects of rural life. These schools and their teachers were added to the rural ways, and the information learned in school was added to the body of superstition in a crazy-quilt pattern which largely remains intact today.

An oral interview with M. Jean Pouch, born in 1891 in Le Devès, Corrèze, revealed a picture of school days and the teacher's habits, some of which were accepted by the community and others which provoked parental opposition. M. Pouch recounted that his teacher was a sickly old man who often dozed off during class. When the children were sure that he was asleep, they paraded about the room having a good time ridiculing the old man. When he awoke, he would punish them, either by beating them or forcing them to kneel on a pile of corn kernels. One time, when the boys were sure he was fast asleep, they took off for the swimming hole and when he awoke he found the room empty after a search of the village, the old teacher finally found the boys and ordered them back to school. The teacher's wrath was taken out on the younger ones. In his fury, the older boys were sure of a beating and hid out for a few days while the teacher tore a boy's jacket. The next day the boy's parents came in to complain of the mistreatment. Though they did not disapprove of corporal punishment, they were angry about the torn jacket.[6]

In the realm of beliefs, peasant communities were often able to absorb new ideas into a growing potpourri of notions. For example, in many rural areas, mothers believed that dirt protected their children's skin; lice were believed to protect babies' heads. P. Sebillot wrote in 1886 that he knew many mothers in the Haute Bretagne who had adopted the rules of hygiene taught in school but, though they combed their children's heads regularly, they made sure to leave three or four lice undisturbed, certain that lice ate bad blood.[7]

Another example of such accommodations can be seen in the

3. A stamp given to pupils

4. School mural: the one who does not work resembles an ass

beliefs surrounding the subject of cutting babies' nails. The custom in many areas was to let the nails grow for at least one year. As teachers and doctors began to advocate cutting the nails much earlier to prevent babies from scratching themselves, a new version of the superstition was heard: "Si une femme coupe les ongles de son enfant le dimanche, l'enfant est sûr de mourir dans l'année." ("If a woman cuts her child's nails on Sunday, the child will surely die within the year").[8]

This flexibility was not the case in the eighteenth century. One enlightened doctor recollected in 1774 that he had raised his own son, as an example to the peasant community, on a strict regime of cold daily baths. Even in winter the baths were icy. The child was never sick, while the unbathed children of the peasants were frequently ill. The local peasants, however, remained firm in their beliefs: "On dit que j'étais bien heureux que mon fils eût résisté à tout ce que j'avais fait pour le tuer." ("They said that I was very lucky that my son had resisted all my efforts to kill him").[9]

Given the greater instability of schools, run by secular instructors, it was not surprising that more and more parents were eager for
their children to go to schools supported by the church. Especially
with regard to girls, the general opinion was that education should
be more religion oriented and that lay *institutrices* were something
of an oddity. Parents were usually willing to transfer their daughters
to a religious school if one would come to their commune. By the
1860s two-thirds of the girls in French primary schools were being
taught by nuns. Only one-fifth of the boys were taught by brothers,
a fact which partly reflected the male secular teacher's greater ability to hold on to his schools, usually by allying himself with the
municipal council and the mayor against the parish priest.[10]

In rural schools lack of teaching materials was the norm. A
map of France, an alphabet, a portrait of the reigning monarch,
were the only distinguishing marks of a country school. Peasant
children brought to school whatever books or papers they had at
home. These were usually deeds or tax papers or petitions which had
been in the family for decades and were, for the most part, much
too difficult for beginning readers. Most of their contents were undoubtedly learned by rote.

The individual method of instruction was most compatible with
these poor materials and was common in the rural schools through
the end of the Second Empire, despite repeated attempts on the part
of inspectors to change to the simultaneous system. In the individual
method, the teacher called pupils to come up to his desk one at a
time. All the others were supposed to be studying quietly while the
instructor worked with the individual student for a few minutes.
The child, who returned to his desk, was then supposed to repeat
quietly what he had learned until his next turn came to recite. This
type of organization led to lack of discipline among the pupils, who
ranged in age from six to ten. Physical punishment was the norm for
misbehavior.

A study of inspectors' reports from 1833 to 1856 provides some
specific examples of these general trends.[11] In 1839, the inspector of
Indre-et-Loire, M. Dehen, sent in a gloomy picture of the situation
of primary schools in his department. The general situation was
worsening, he reported, because of the low pay offered to teachers;
some schools had closed and there were fewer children attending

school in 1839 than there were in 1835. Among the 151 teachers, 15 were provisionally licensed women who taught mixed (boys and girls) classes because no one else would take the job. Six nonlicensed women were also teaching in 1839.

Dehen tried to analyze the problems in his area. First of all, he reasoned, the population of the department was low and that made it difficult to fill a school with children.[12] Second, land was held in small plots by farmers who were too poor to pay for the education of their sons and daughters even though they were land owners. Further, the religious and civic leaders of the department were indifferent, if not hostile, to educating the poor.

The result was that insufficient funds were voted for education. In 1840 the department voted 45,592 fr. for primary schools. Dehen judged this sum to be paltry, given the need to open 95 new public schools (see Table 1).

Table 1

A. Status of Primary Education

Number of communes which should have schools	248
Number of communes which have public schools	153
Number of communes which have only private schools	24
Number of communes which have no schools	71
Number of communes which should establish public schools	95

B. Expenditures for Primary Education

General supplement	16,000
Grant to communes for the acquisition of school buildings	24,000
Grant to buy and renovate school furniture	1,500
Payment for teachers who went to normal schools	1,400
Aid to girls' schools	2,000
	45,592

Dehen went on to describe the needs. Classrooms were lacking in space for any sort of movement. Air and light were also lacking in these rooms. With the exception of three, the mixed schools were without partitions and without separate entrances for boys and girls. Some schools had only one outhouse for the use of both sexes. It would take twenty years, Dehen estimated, for the department to have sufficient classrooms and classroom furniture.

There were equally great needs with regard to improving instruction among the 315 teachers in the department who were divided as follows: 156 male communal teachers, 44 male private teachers, 26 female communal teachers, 89 female private teachers. Dehen held private teachers in low esteem generally. "Those one finds in the country are generally incompetent. The local authorities tolerate them or even encourage them to stay. The municipal councils keep them at the level of private instructor in order to keep from hiring a public instructor. Often these are former school masters who keep a few students around to, as they say, "avoid boredom."

With regard to teachers in girls' schools, of the 89 private positions, 17 were held by religious sisters, 72 by nonreligious. Dehen confirmed the general trend mentioned above: "Most of the female lay instructors languish in poverty; the female instructors from religious orders lack for nothing." The nuns only take positions in the rich communes and those which are more populous. From such communes they receive aid or presents from people who share their philosophy or who are truly moved by the piety which attaches itself to the clergy. In addition, the nuns have the support of the curé, the man who carries the most weight with the mothers of the families when they decide to send their daughters to school.

Dehen concluded that it was not surprising that schools run by the sisters were generally much better than those run by secular teachers. The former had good preparation for their jobs and close supervision. They were obliged to submit lesson plans, to attend summer classes designed to improve their teaching ability, and to use uniform texts, while the secular teachers had none of the above advantages and were, moreover, obliged to change their jobs frequently.

One of the reasons for frequent job changes was the low salary paid to teachers. Dehen estimated that two-thirds of the male public school teachers were impoverished. The same year as Dehen's report, 1839, the inspector of the Oise calculated a table of teachers' salaries which further illustrated the desperate position of most teachers whose mean income was approximately 500 francs per year; the median was 371.

Table 2 Teachers with Annual Income (in francs)

Number of Teachers	Income
4	1500 plus
9	1200–1500
27	900–1200
160	600–900
133	500–600
168	400–500
185	300–400
56	under 300

In a similar report from the Vosges, the inspector reported the average income for men: 487 fr., and for women: 380 fr.[14] This can be compared to the national average daily wage for laborers: 2 frs. for men and 1 fr. for women.

In the inspector's report from Corrèze of 1841, there was an urgent plea to establish minimum wages for women teachers. This was immediately necessary, he explained, because of 150 girls' schools in the department, 114 were illegal and had no chance to survive. Further, "these teachers offered the families no guarantee either of abilities or of suitability." And in the religious girls' schools, which made up the bulk of the remainder, the inspector was not permitted to enter the school to see what was going on. In the inspector's judgment: "this is an abuse, a disorder which must be repressed."[15]

Even in the better-off department of Haute-Loire, the situation of women teachers was abysmal. Of 654 teaching in 1842, 574 had neither license nor letter of obedience. They were teaching because of "the tolerance and the need of the population." The inspector complained that these secular women had no normal school to go to. The religious sisters belonged to seventeen different congregations, only some of which were able to train teachers well.[16]

Two years later, the inspector of the department of Nevers provided a description of the standing of each woman teacher in his district.[17] A brief sampling showed the diversity of conditions. Fremiot, Marie Joseph, was a nun who earned 800 francs per year. She was rated as follows: morality — good; ability — sufficient; zeal — considerable; relations with the priest and the mayor — good. By contrast, Mariet, Pauline, was a single lay teacher who earned

400 francs per annum. The inspector classified her school as: "espèce d'asile privée" ("a type of private shelter"). Cardinaux, Marie Madeleine, was a widow who earned 350 francs per year despite a reputation for very good morality, sufficient ability, great zeal and excellent relations with the commune. At the other extreme, Bressat, Marie, a married woman, kept a pension which earned her 4,000 francs per year. Lack of uniformity was the rule!

Commencing in March 1850, every French commune with a population of 800 or more, was obliged by the Falloux Law to have a primary school for girls. In 1856, Inspector Gerard from Toul reported that in his department the law was being followed even in communes of 700 people.[18] Indeed, he added, a definite change in attitude had taken place in the preceding few years; people now wanted to support girls' education. There was also unanimity of opinion on the preferred type of school for girls:

In Toul we believe that the woman teacher should be a member of a religious community because she thus inspires more confidence and she is often more devoted to her work because she does not have to think about material necessities which a nonreligious teacher would have to think about.

This positive attitude on the part of the people of Toul was probably influenced by the fact that fourteen communes enjoyed the benefits of foundations; legacies from a previous century which favored girls' education. As a result of this aid the communes were able to open schools early, without having to resort to extraordinary sacrifices on the part of the population. The total annual revenue from these donations amounted to 4,219 francs and was used to maintain buildings and pay teachers. By contrast, in the department of Finistère, the inspector reported changed attitudes on the part of the population but, though there was general approval of the idea of providing schools for girls, they were very few in number and many of them were still of very poor quality.[19]

The need to construct schools was the major capital expenditure required for public schools in Finistère; in 1856, only four buildings set aside for schools belonged to the communes; nine were rented (only two of which were judged suitable by the inspector); two were borrowed. In two communes girls were relegated to a corner in a boys' school. Private schools were divided sharply between those which taught in French and those which taught in Breton. The former had very good classrooms while the latter had very bad rooms—smoky, dirty, full of inappropriate furniture. Tables, blackboards, and books were also lacking in most of the public schools. For a detailed comparison of teachers, pupils, and schools in two departments, see Appendix B.

Even before the Guizot Law was passed, the question of why some areas of France had more schools and higher literacy rates than others had been raised by the economist, Baron Dupin. In 1826, he charted the growth of primary schools and concluded that in areas where industry was developed and population was dense, instruction was likely to be widespread.[20] More recently, Michel Fleury and Pierre Valmary established that climate, language, religion, and other social factors were significant in determining whether an area would support or oppose primary schools.[21] Additional variables have been suggested by this study. The experience of the locality with the national government on such issues as road building, taxes, and the draft would be likely to predispose a community to trust or distrust national officials with regard to schools.

Of even greater significance might be the existence of dame schools in the area before the new teachers came to the village. Where old schools performed to community satisfaction, there might be less willingness to send children to schools taught by outsiders. Inspectors frequently bemoaned the quality of the dame schools, but evolving as they did from the community's needs and teaching community values, they were not scorned by parents or children. Reports from inspectors from all over France included references to the tenacious survival of dame schools throughout the Second Empire.[22]

There is some evidence to suggest that parents who learned to read and write in a limited way in dame schools were more likely to encourage the growth of primary schools taught by more highly trained teachers. As has been pointed out in a study on Japanese education, at the very least, literacy constitutes training in being trained.[23] Thus, parents who had submitted to some process of disciplined and conscious learning were more likely to respond to further training in later life for themselves and for their children.

Despite significant regional variations due to different levels of industrialization, different experiences with the national government, and differing traditions, the overriding impression produced by a study of primary schools in France from 1830–1880 is that of steady growth. Charts one and two show, in a forty-year period, the number of schools grew from 30,796 to 53,820, while the population climbed from 32 to 38 million. Simultaneously, the illiteracy rate declined steadily. As we shall see in the next chapter, socialization for modern adult roles commenced with the teaching of the ABCs.[24]

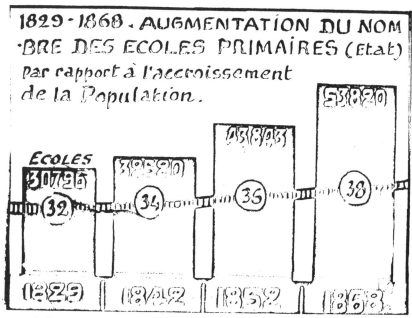

La ligne transversale indique en millions d'hab. la progression de la population francaise

GROWTH OF NUMBER OF PRIMARY SCHOOLS COMPARED
TO GROWTH IN FRENCH POPULATION

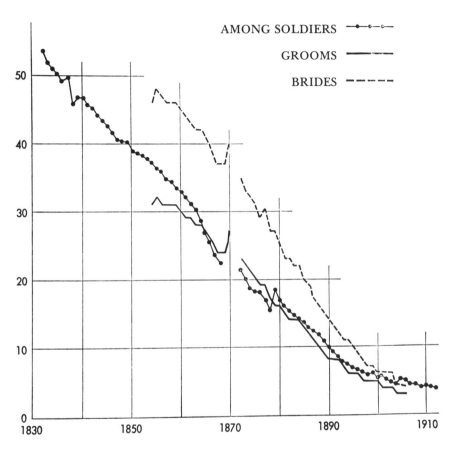

PERCENTAGE OF ILLITERATES,
1830-1914

CHAPTER TWO

The ABCs in the Guizot System

The simultaneous method which involved teaching the whole class at the same time from the same text was begun by the Brothers of the Christian Doctrine and spread slowly to all other primary schools. It was a natural outgrowth of religious catechismal training. One of the most popular texts was Fleury's *Catéchisme historique*, which began as follows:

God made the world from nothing by His words and His will and for His glory. He did it in six days. The first day He created the heaven and the earth; then light; the second day He created the firmament which He called the sky; the third day He separated the water from the land, and made the earth bring forth the plants; on the fourth He made the sun, the moon and the stars; on the fifth He made the birds in the air and the fish in the sea; on the sixth He made animals on the earth and made man in His image; and God rested on the seventh day.

Question: Who made the world?
Answer: God did.
Q: What did He make it from?
A: From nothing.
Q: How did He make it?
A: By His word.
Q: Why did He make it?
A: For His glory.
Q: In how many days did God create the world?
A: In six days.
Q: What did He make on the first day?

A: The heaven and the earth, later the light.
Q: And the second day?
A: The firmament which He called sky.
Q: What did He do on the third day?
A: He separated the water from the land and brought forth all sorts of plants.
Q: And the fourth day?
A: He created the sun, the moon, and the stars.
Q: And the fifth?
A: He made the birds in the air and the fish in the sea.
Q: And the sixth?
A: He made all the earth's animals and made man in His image.
Q: And on the seventh day?
A: After making all the things, He rested.[1]

The text was presented; the questions were asked; the answers were given. Different questions, alternative answers had no place in the classrooms created by the Loi Guizot. This *mentalité* was not limited to religious instruction, which authorities agreed was the main purpose of primary schools, but permeated all other areas as well.

The Brothers also divided primary instruction into three different levels: reading, writing, and grammar; spelling; and arithmetic. This method required the use of three instructors and was too expensive for most French primary schools until the end of the nineteenth century. A modified version of this method, the mutual method, was invented in England where it had much success, but it was never widespread in France. In the mutual method, monitors were chosen from the best pupils in the class to teach less advanced students, while the teacher supervised the larger group. Guizot endorsed the simultaneous method, which he thought had the best chance of meeting his educational goals: giving French children some basic knowledge while creating national unity and social stability:

The spirit and unity of the French nation is spread when the French language and the sytem of checks and balances is taught throughout the land. Finally, the teaching of moral and religious principles provides for another level of needs. These needs are as real as the aforementioned and Providence has put them in the hearts of rich and poor alike to enhance life and protect the social order.[2]

These general goals were elaborated in the rules for primary schools established in each town and village. For example, in the Croix-Rousse, a suburb of Lyon, rules for primary schools were organized into forty-one articles and published in 1838.[3]. Article one urged teachers to follow the simultaneous method or the mutual method, or a combination of the two. Those who still taught by the individual method were urged to abandon it with the shortest possible delay, since it was prejudicial and even dangerous for the moral health of students. Article three stressed the need for uniform textbooks and article four, uniform standards for promotion. National standards of uniform spelling and pronounciation were emphasized.

A large section of the rules was related to moral instruction; teachers were reminded to inculcate principles of religion and to teach pupils their duties to society. Specific obligations on the part of children to parents were a favorite theme of those who wrote children's books. The work of T. H. Barrau, pseudonym for Louis d'Altemont, can serve as an example. In 1837, Barrau, who was the principal of the college of Chaumont, wrote *Des Devoirs des Enfants envers leurs parents.* In it he reminded children: "L'Enfant à tout âge doit honneur et respect à ses père et mère; il est soumis à leur autorité jusqu'à ce qu'il soit devenu majeur" ("The child of any age owes his father and mother both honor and respect; he must bow to their authority until he has reached his majority"). Barrau emphasized the qualities of submission, obedience and love of parents. Barrau also recognized the need for different types of education for girls and boys.

Boys, thought Barrau and his contemporaries, were brought up for diverse careers. Women, for one: "plaire à leur maris, diriger leur maison, soigner les enfants" ("to please their husband, to run the house, to care for the children"). He went on to explain:

The young boy belongs to his country and it is for the country that the family rears him. A young girl belongs to the family: to that of her parents, at first, then, to that which she adopts and then, to that which she forms. It is, therefore, the family's duty to surround her with great care and to raise her with love within the intimacy of family life.[4]

Barrau's moralizing literature did not make exciting reading for young children, especially when it was accompanied by the widespread *Bible de Royaumont, Conduite, Psautier, Telémaque,* and *Grammaire de Lhomond.* Newer books written in the 1830s and '40s were frequently about children of artistocratic families. *Le Moraliste du jeune âge* by A. Antoine de Saint Gervais, published in 1835, is a good example. The book commenced with an introduction about the Melval family. M. Melval had the bad fortune to lose his cherished wife, which left him a widower with three tenderly loved children; two boys and a girl. Enjoying a huge fortune, he wanted to give his children an appropriate education, especially since he could assist in their training. During the vacation period he promised his little family that he would take them to their chateau because it was more amusing there than in the city. Edmond and Caroline reminded their father of his promise.

"That's right," he said to them, "I wanted to surprise you by taking you there tomorrow; I've already given the orders for that very purpose. Your fine conduct has answered my hopes. I am satisfied with your hard work and it is now my pleasant duty to reward you."

But then, addressing himself directly to Charles, M. Melval asked him if he had anything to reproach himself for. "Have you merited the respect of your instructors like your brother Edmond? Your sister too, younger than you, surpasses you with her rapid progress. Do you want to become a lazy oaf?"

Charles, quite shamed by this just reprimand, lowered his eyes like a repentant criminal; he dared not speak. His brother and sister spoke up and implored their father's pardon for him; Charles was moved to tears and he threw himself at his father's feet, all the while promising to make up for his wrongs. "I shall try to forget the unhappiness you have caused me," replied M. Melval, "but if you don't study with more zeal I will leave you alone in town the next time in order to make up your work."

The little family embraced M. Melval with great tenderness and each one happily looked forward to the pleasures which lay ahead.[5]

The rest of the book was a collection of moralizing tales told by the father to his children while on vacation. For example, "Le Jeune Bertrand" showed that laziness was an evil which led to all others, while obeying parents and teachers would lead to a good life. "Les Bons Enfants" lamented the fate of the nobility after the "civil disorders." The stories also illustrated sex-role differentiation. In "Bloise," boys ran and jumped to develop agility and strength while girls practiced virtues of good housekeeping (which would lead to a good marriage). Furthermore, there were several stories dealing specifically with boys: "Eugène et Gustave" (work is honorable), "Adolphe et Théodore" (dangers of gambling), "Paul et Benjamin" (love, honor and obey parents) and "Vincent et Joseph" (need for acquiring a well-rounded education), while only one, "Cécile et Julie" (virtue of earning one's living industriously, living frugally under parental guidance), related specifically to girls.[6]

Some books, like *La Vie Réelle* by Mme. Bourdon, which was praised very highly by the *Journal des Instituteurs*, addressed a bourgeois audience. A few lines will indicate the values which were being taught. Isabelle, the wife of an entrepreneur, was speaking:

We pass our evenings with the family, sometimes at Albert's (Isabelle's brother) home and sometimes in our home. The hours fly by deliciously when we are in such dear company; among our children whose minds and characters are still forming and whose youth adds to the charm of these gatherings . . . During our evenings together Robert (Isabelle's son) reads the classics, especially Virgil, upon which he lovingly comments. Adolphe (Isabelle's nephew), not a very good humanist, translates from the English; Léonce (young son) and Georges (cousin) study their lessons or play a game on a table set up with dominoes, checkers, cards, picture books and crayons. My sister-in-law, Antoinette (Isabelle's daughter), and I work; I do tapestry with large stitches, because of my weakened eyesight and Henriette, who has the eyes of a 15-year-old, does Gobelins, a magnificent chasuble, a masterpeice of taste and patience. Our husbands converse, read, or play chess; at 8 o'clock we take tea; Antoinette plays the piano and we leave without regretting in the least the get-togethers or the brilliant soirées of high society.[7]

Bourdon's portrait of middle-class tranquility and repose, and family cohesiveness was presented as "Real Life." The pictures which follow illustrated family life in another book of the genre, Julie Gourand's *Le Livre de Maman*.[8] The implicit message of these books was that those who didn't achieve middle-class conditions had only themselves to blame. But by mid-century, after sufficient exposure by teachers and inspectors to rural life, there was a new emphasis on writing school books particularly for children from impoverished backgrounds. After all, the middle-class authors did not really expect the rural children to be able to imitate middle-class life

5. The first spoonful

6. Making preserves

7. Mother and daughter

8. At the piano

in every respect. After the Revolution of 1848, they were more careful about the exact meaning of modern life for the poor.

In one of the most widely read books of the period, *Francinet: Principles généraux de la morale, de l'agriculture*, by G. Bruno, pseudonym for Mme. Alfred Fouillée, messages were addressed to poor children.

If one gets into the habit of playing all the time, work becomes very painful and the games eventually become boring. But, if you get into the habit of working, the work gradually becomes more and more agreeable to you and then you reward yourself with a little play.[9]

Francinet was a poor boy who was employed at the age of nine as a spinner by M. Clertan, who had a granddaughter, Aimée, of the same age. Aimée taught Francinet to plan ahead. She explained that it was prudent to think of all possible consequences of one's deeds and never put off acting when you can do something right away. Finally, she concluded, man was made for progress and he was propelled, by suffering, to act. When Aimée asked her tutor why there were no women inventors she was told, "Women don't study science. They are important as mothers of future inventors."

The role of mothers in educating their children is addressed with great clarity in a significant book for rural teachers by J. M. Dalimier, an assistant inspector for primary instruction in the department of Ille-et-Vilaine. "Each pupil has as first teacher his mother who is charged with the initiation of the child into social life: "forming his heart, his mind and his character."[10] "But," Dalimier continued, "we should not fool ourselves. In the countryside the education of the family is, in general, faulty or incomplete. Few mothers appreciate the importance of educating their children. Furthermore," Dalimier asked, "how many mothers are there whose every moment isn't absorbed with providing the physical necessities for their family?" Dalimier concluded with the following admonition to rural teachers, "You, on whom the parents bestow their most precious possessions, know how to inspire within your students the love of obedience. There should be no resistance to the tasks you ask them to perform." Thus, along with the articulation of new values for rural children, came a new parent, the teacher, who had the time and presumably the skill to inculcate these new values.

Dalimier was specific in his instructions to teachers destined for rural areas. Their job was to change a culture—to banish from the home and from the classroom all fairy tales, stories of wolves and wild spirits and to substitute for these stories, the "truth." The latter was a combination of Catholic beliefs and acceptance of middle-class standards of cleanliness and orderliness. "Get your students to be orderly; all of their assignments should be done with attention and exactitude; the lessons which they follow with submission will make them understand the sacredness of duty and will give them the habit of working."

Dalimier also wanted the teachers to change the health standards of the countryside. Not only were stories of wild spirits to be banished from the homes of pupils, but so were incurable infirmities which were widespread in rural areas and, in Dalimier's view, due to the shameful disorder and neglect in rural houses. Dalimier charged teachers, "You must penetrate into those narrow and dark homes to remove disorder." It is significant that Dalimier spoke primarily to women teachers whom he saw as appropriate culture carriers to the countryside. This widespread view was also expressed by Boulay de Meurthe in the Chamber of Deputies; "Législateurs, vous ne faites que lois, les femmes font des moeurs. ("Legislators, you only make the laws, women make the customs").[11]

Along with disorder and stories of wild creatures, dirt was to be banished from rural children. Cleanliness was, for the middle class, a precursor to self-control in all aspects of life. "Cleanliness leads to ideas of decency and habits of order; it helps to inspire the respect of man for himself. It accustoms us to vigilance over ourselves; it commands moderation, attention and, limiting ourselves in many ways, it disposes us to work." Teachers in rural areas should be aware that their pupils would be frequently arriving in the classroom covered with mud. Children who must walk to school on lanes full of water must be forced to clean their clothing and warm their bodies before they could begin school work. These habits would begin to uproot the erroneous peasant belief that children were born with such good health that cold weather, hunger, thirst, or lack of sleep would not make them ill.

By 1843, when Dalimier's book came out, ten years had passed since the passage of the Guizot Law. There was now sufficient

evidence from rural schools for Dalimier to point out several problem areas. Many teachers, he was convinced, had enough knowledge
but didn't know how to teach. The caricature of the rural
schoolmaster walking down a muddy lane reciting Cicero was well
known. Dalimier advised: "Imagine yourselves in the bosom of your
students' families; follow them through their daily chores . . . by
such means you will learn to devise a method of teaching, better
than anything you might learn from books." Since most rural pupils
would continue to live in the countryside, teachers were advised to
instruct them in useful skills such as keeping accounts and buying
and selling crops.

Specialized teaching for rural children was extended to
pedagogical methods. Dalimier emphasized the inappropriateness
of rote education for rural pupils. He set forward the following example of teaching:

Teacher: What am I holding in my hand?
Pupil: A piece of glass.
Teacher: Examine it and tell me its properties.
Pupil: It is cold.
Teacher: Touch it; compare it to your sponge.
Pupil: The glass is polished and hard.
Teacher: Is there more glass in the room?
Pupil: Yes, the windows.
Teacher: (Closing the blinds), can you see out?
Pupil: No.
Teacher: Why?
Pupil: The blinds are shutting out the view.
Teacher: Then what would you say about glass?
Pupil: We can see through it.
Teacher: Can you give me a name for this quality?
Pupil: No.
Teacher: I'm going to tell you. Note it: Transparent. What idea do
you have now of a thing that is transparent?
Pupil: That you can see through it.
Teacher: Tell me something else that is transparent.
Pupil: Water.
Teacher: If I drop the glass or throw a stone at the window, what
will happen?
Pupil: The glass will break; it is fragile.
Teacher: What are fragile objects, then?
Pupil: Those which break easily.[12]

Nevertheless, most teachers continued to use the old methods because they were taught in normal schools run by religious orders that adhered to catechismal teaching. Religious and civil authorities seemed more concerned with correcting the "bad habits" of the poor than with teaching children to think. In addition to the concern about dirt and disorder, clergy, like Chanoine Ponceau, introduced the fear of cabarets, lack of religious devotion, and the spirit of independence. The need to temper adaptation to modernity with acceptance of humble status became increasingly evident in the manuals of the 1850s. Ponceau urged:

Teach your pupils to love and respect the status and ways of their parents; the simple life, the honorable and happy life of the laboring peasant. Teach them to watch out for the dangerous temptation of leaving the village for the city. How many have been misled and continue to be every day! Instead of finding the comfort of which they dreamed, they find, more often than not, poverty, corruption and frequently, dishonor.[13]

Unfulfilled dreams of the good life led to problems other than drinking, as Ponceau and the whole generation of 1848 were well aware. By the late 50s educators were being urged to temper the spirit of independence, once seen as important to laissez-faire economic society, with a corresponding notion of duty to the nation which implied deference to the status quo:

Finally, there is an evil in our society to which you must direct all your attention. It is more pervasive and may lead to more disastrous consequences. It is the spirit of independence which today reigns everywhere among our youth. As a result, the principle of authority has been considerable weakened. Fight this spirit of independence and reestablish authority with all the zeal you can muster. To that end, accustom your children at an early age to bend to the yoke of obedience and discipline. Always speak of authority with the greatest show of deference and never allow your children, either in word or deed, to show a lack of respect to those representatives of civil or ecclesiastic authority.[14]

In 1858, when Ponceau wrote his *Manuel de l'instituteur et de l'institutrice*, he echoed the Guizot philosophy of 1833: the goal of education was to cultivate the individual and thereby improve society at large. Ponceau concurred with Guizot that education was the best means for establishing order, peace, religion, and the proper respect for authority. But Ponceau's book also reflected the decades of resistance and inertia experienced by those who tried to put Guizot's plan into action. Thus Ponceau explained, "For education to have a truly efficacious influence on society, it must unify two conditions . . . It must direct its opposition to the abuses and disorders which reign in our society . . . it must be strong enough to fortify children against these abuses and disorders."[15] These were two difficult conditions to meet as Guizot and his successors discovered.

More and more as the century wore on, as greater numbers of children attended primary school, inspectors, teachers, and school book authors came to rely on rural mothers to act as the ambassadors of limited aspects of middle-class culture to peasant families. By the end of the century mother had become omnipresent in children's literature, while father's role had greatly diminished. Mother became a constant aid, guide, and moral and emotional support; she became "La Petite Mère."

> At night when off to sleep I go,
> Who comes to hug me?
> Who smiles when I awaken?
> It's you, little mother.
>
> Who scolds in such a tender voice
> that I repent of things if only to
> hear that tenderness?
> It's you, little mother.
>
> When old age overtakes you.
> My turn will come to give you aid,
> Who then will offer tenderness?
> It's me, little mother.[16]

In Louis Peigné's *Recitation à l'école primaire*, the chapter on family commenced with the above verse and continued with verses entitled, "Le Lever de l'Enfant," "Le Petit Frère," "Grande Soeur," "Quoique petit," and "Ceux que j'aime." Father had all but disappeared from the family. Though Peigné thought that fathers should befriend their children, they clearly played a minor role in their children's lives. Peigné suggested that fathers should be affectionate to their children early in the morning (before leaving for work). Only in the last verse was father's real function in the family described:

> I love daddy, all week long he
> goes off to work to earn bread for me.[17]

These ideas which emphasized the dichotomy between family and work, and between men's and women's roles, were alien to the rural way of life. Though peasants knew gender role differentiations, they were not based on middle class division of labor and myths of the perfect mother and father. Peasant women were accustomed to active participation in the economic life of the family. Peasant fathers were accustomed to being equally concerned with the family's well-being as were their spouses. Both men and women in the countryside distrusted and resisted the new ways being brought in with the ABCs.

CHAPTER THREE

Overcoming Parental Opposition to Education

In 1856 the inspector of primary school education in Toul reported that ninety-seven girls of school age were not attending any classes nor receiving instruction at home. The main reason that girls in his department did not go to school was that they were employed doing embroidery or making lace. He commented: "It is painful to think that many of these girls are obliged to work from morning to night in the company of persons who frequently are not reserved in their conversation; in dirty, dark, humid rooms lacking in fresh air and space."[1] Were the girls deprived of an education out of dire necessity to put food on the table for the family? Not in the opinion of the inspector, who believed that greed motivated parents to drive their daughters to this hard work for exploitative wages. But, the company deplored by the inspector were the girls' mothers, sisters, aunts, grandmothers and neighbors, and the conditions he found intolerable were not different from those which they endured in their homes. The wages he found exploitative might well have meant the difference between satiety and hunger.

The inspector of the Ariège, in 1836, understood that there were many causes which made parents opposed to educating their children, but the most difficult to uproot was the habit of ignorance and the conviction of many peasants that it was possible to get along sufficiently well, even to have a happy life, without any book learning.[2] Fifteen years later school authorities from the same department still found stiff resistance to school attendance.[3]

It is important to note that peasant parents were not opposed to learning as such; they were opposed to sending their children to schools brought in by authorities from outside the community whose values and purposes, and in some cases even language, were different and suspect. In the Midi, the study and use of the French language were considered ridiculous and of no use whatsoever. Instructors were forced to teach in patois or not at all. Even in 1893, according to official figures, about a quarter of the 37,000-odd communes in France spoke no French. Their population accounted for seven and a half million out of the thirty million people in France. About half a million out of four million children between seven and thirteen spoke no French; another million and a half could speak or understand but could not write it—a strong suggestion that they knew it badly. And, the reports of Academy inspectors, inspecting Teachers' Normal Schools through the 1870s and 1880s, showed that the children's teachers and apprentice teachers knew it badly too.[4]

Patois	Français
Quand tu viens comḿ no à nos pais tu peux biai d'veser	Quand tu viens comme ça à notre pays tu peux bien parler comme on fait
comme on fait ichi, tu sais biai qu'o diro: baie do ch' tcio, pach'qui d'meur' à l' ville i fait biai d'l'imbaro!	ici tu sais bien qu'on dira: regarde donc celui là parcequ'il demeure à la ville il fait bien de l'embarras!

Sample Patois Spoken in Oise 1835[5]

In sum, French remained a foreign language for a large minority of the country's inhabitants. Almost half of the children who reached adulthood in the last quarter of the nineteenth century were taught French, if and when they were taught it at all, as a foreign language. Speaking French was a symbol of social promotion. French reflected a superior otherness, like that of the squire, or priest, or teacher and would be accepted by peasants only when social mobility was something that made sense to them. In some areas it came early in the century, as can be seen from a story told by Albert Dauzat about the peasants in Puy-de-Dome who began to give their children French names, in imitation of their local squires. Around 1820, the priest of Vic-le-Comte asked a little girl her name: "Marie," she said.

"Marie! But that is a young lady's name, not a name for a peasant. You may be called Miyette or Mayon."

And the little girl answered, "I'm as entitled to bear the Holy Virgin's name as any lady." [6]

French, as Eugen Weber pointed out, was dignified, suspect, and superior. It was also urban, modern, and "civilized." It provided the terminology of innovation and modernity, and it provided certain more or less abstract notions for which traditional language had no terms. Similarly, in the area of mathematics, peasants opposed the teaching of arithmetic in school because few of them could count, even fewer could figure. Tallysticks were the common means of keeping track of bills for bakers and innkeepers. While schools were introducing the metric system and all the official measurements, peasants clung to traditional measures like the *toise* (about 6 ft.), the *pouce* (inch), the *league* (about 3 miles), calculated firewood in *cordes* (bundles), and quoted prices in *pistoles* or *écus* (3 frs.). The acceptance of these new measures marked a rite of passage from "Peasants into Frenchmen." [7]

Peasant children were not uneducated. They learned from their own parents much that was valuable to survival in their culture and to the perpetuation of the ways of life accepted by their families. In some regions girls learned at very young ages to do embroidery which was not only complicated, requiring great manual dexterity and memory of design patterns, but also required stamina and concentration.[8] Boys in some regions learned to make musical instruments, that demanded great precision and attention. Children in all regions learned at tender ages a variety of tasks associated with farm life, including skills and responsibilities for punctuality and accuracy which might have astounded middle-class school inspectors. Many communes had some exposure to schools and book learning before the national government came in to establish them. These early schools, described by the inspectors of French schools in 1833, shed some more light on the relative importance peasant parents attached to book learning.

In many areas, school was really a baby-sitting operation and teachers received no more prestige than shepherds. Their wages were so low that they would have to have another occupation or go begging to supplement their teachers' salaries. In Landes, "Instituteur et mendiant est presque synonyme" ("Teacher and beggar are almost synonymous").[9] Many teachers were handicapped — either deaf, epileptic, missing limbs, or else they were habitual drunks. They were, for the most part, local men or women who were kept alive by the small supplementary wage they received for minding the children. In 1842, a Sister reported from the small hamlet of Chenelette:

In almost all of Chenelette there lived servants who taught classes while spinning wool; each woman did what she could to attract the richest pupils. That is to say, those who might pay the modest sum of 60-75 centimes a month.

In many rural regions there were also annual visits of from two to four months of teachers who were more educated and hardworking. Most came from families of itinerant teachers and were Béarnais, Piémontais, Brianconnais, or Auvernats. With these teachers the peasants would have the upper hand and would frequently haggle over terms of employment. As one contended: "You're not worth much as an instructor and if it's necessary to pay the 200 francs that we just voted (for educational purposes), we would prefer your competitor. But, there is a way to work things out. For example, if you could furnish the school room gratis and allow us to dispense with paying any additional expenses for your lodging, then the position is all yours." [10]

In sum, it is clear that book learning and school were peripheral to peasant life and that outsiders were suspect and had to convince the peasants that they had something worthwhile to teach. The degree of opposition can be measured not only by anecdotal accounts recorded by inspectors, but also by data that they tabulated throughout the mid-nineteenth century until primary education became not merely recommended, but compulsory in the 1880s. Table 3 is an example of the data from the Corrèze in 1847, fourteen years after the Guizot Law was passed.

Table 3. Number of Primary School Aged Children Not Going to School in Corrèze, 1847 [11]

Name of Commune	Population	Boys Primary Schools	Primary School age Children Not In School	Number of children who do not attend primary school for one of the following reasons						School Drop-outs
				Physical Disabilities	Long Distances and Poor Roads	Insufficient Classroom Space	Poverty	No Schools Available	Parental Indifference	
Brive	113,581	80	10,999	35	2,205	3,288	2,069	1,487	1,915	656
Tulle	130,853	90	13,701	76	2,578	3,378	2,857	2,273	2,539	660
Ussel	62,046	45	6,120	24	1,321	1,390	1,173	1,439	773	183
TOTALS	306,480	215	30,820	135	6,104	8,056	6,099	5,199	5,227	1,499

As we have already described in chapter two, resistance to primary schools and book learning was not equally strong in all areas of France. Even within the same department there were often important differences in the willingness of communes to accept the Guizot system. In 1833, the Recteur of the Academy of Toulouse reported such a division between the population of the mountains and those of the plains:

It seems to me that a great division cuts two mighty swaths between the meridional populations: the regions and towns of the plains and those of the mountains. That is to say, the rich areas and the poor. This division combines with two others which almost always follow suit . . . the agricultural regions and the industrial: the Catholic areas and the Protestant, or those in which one finds both cults cohabitating. Almost everywhere, the Protestants inhabit the mountains and almost everywhere, one finds that industry follows them. The most profound ignorance joined to a complete indifference to education covers the plains like a vast cloud from the last foothill of the Pyrénées to Foix in Arièges etc . . . Toulouse is in the center of this great cloud like a beacon of light which is unable to pierce through the shadows.[12]

Three years later, a new inspector from the same department explained the underlying reason for this division: "Communes which need business and technology to help them procure the resources which the soil denies them appreciate the benefits of education. But, those which are solely concerned with the cultivation of their land and the care of their animals feel no good accruing from education or instruction." [13]

Thus, in areas where land was too poor to support the population, or where topographical conditions encouraged commerce and industry rather than agriculture, learning to read, write, and cipher was appreciated because it helped the inhabitants in their daily pursuits. In those areas where commerce led to interaction with other departments or even other nations, different cultures and various ways of solving problems were more familiar than in agricultural communes where local dialects prevented communication among neighboring communes.[14] Perhaps, acceptance of different ways was a precursor to acceptance of the modern idea of change. What is certain is that it made the commercial and industrial commune more receptive to the Guizot Law.

If the peasants remained uninterested in change, how could the school officials, who were convinced of the need to change peasants, accomplish their task? The inspectors, who in many cases, were personally opposed to involving the church in education, especially for their own sons and daughters, increasingly came to believe that the church alone could handle the peasants' reluctance to send children to school. As one put it in 1852: "We are counting quite heavily on the active and enlightened participation of the clergy to vanquish, and triumph over old customs and superstitions." [15]

In the same year, Cardinal Donnet, Archbishop of Bordeaux, sounded this clarion call in his pastoral letter: "In schools and through schools we shall prepare the return to faith, to family life, to good morals." [16] This became the rallying cry which was used to bring the peasants into primary schools during the next fifty years. Thus, peasants went to the new schools, not to learn to read and to write and to do arithmetic, though in many cases those skills were taught in passing, but rather to return to religion. Mothers were especially influenced by parish priests who withheld communion from children who did not go to school.

From its inception, the Guizot system had relied on the church to provide the appropriate moral values to accompany primary education. Guizot explained to the Chamber of Deputies in 1833: "What is needed is that the general atmosphere of the school should be moral and religious. Intellectual development allied to moral and religious development is a fine thing, but when it is isolated . . . it becomes a source of pride, lack of discipline and selfishness and is, in consequence, dangerous to society." [17] But, during the July Monarchy, the main preoccupation of the church had been with secondary education because this seemed to provide the key to the general political situation. If the church educated the voting public (which was then restricted to middle-class males) to Catholic beliefs, it could expect to succeed in regaining its ancient position of authority in the French state. Peasant and worker children had to wait until after the debacle of 1848 for church authorities to take them more seriously.

By the time the Falloux Law, which greatly expanded the authority of the church over education, was passed in March 1850, whatever liberal opposition to Catholic influence over primary education had existed as a residue from the eighteenth century enlightenment ideas had been overcome by the fear of the uncontrolled mob. Adolphe Thiers, at one time a leading proponent of the church, penned a nearly universal sentiment:

Today, when all social ideas are somewhat perverted, and when one plans on giving each village an instructor who will be a Fourierist, I regard the curé as an indispensable arbiter of the people's ideas; it is he who will teach them, at least in the name of Christ, that suffering is a condition of life. Therefore, when the poor catch cold, they will no longer think it was the rich who gave it to them.[18]

Not only was the bourgeoisie prepared to hand over primary education to the church as the most effective way of keeping the people in a state of social discipline, but the church, now that suffrage was extended to all men, was increasingly prepared to accept this responsibility. The decade following the passage of the Falloux Law witnessed a large growth in the number of teaching orders as well as increasing control of the church over the education of lay teachers through the creation of religious normal schools. While the church had concentrated on the big cities and on the education of the bourgeoisie before 1848, after the "Springtime of the People" the church penetrated every primary school.

During the July Monarchy, the government had refused to recognize the right of new religious orders to teach, but beginning in 1851, Louis Napoleon passed laws encouraging a spectacular growth of those orders:

June 1851	— Petits Frères de Marie (Loire)
November 1851	— Petits Frères de Marie (Rhône)
May 1853	— Frères de Saint-Joseph (Rhône)
May 1854	— Frères de Saint-François d'Assise (Charente-Inférieure)
May 1854	— Frères de la Croix de Jésus (Ain)
August 1856	— Frères de Saint François Régis (Haute-Loire)
September 1865	— Frères des Ecoles Chrétiennes de la Miséricorde (Manche)[19]

With regard to women's orders, the state was even more encouraging; between 1852 and 1859, 923 congregations of women were granted the right to teach (some were older congregations which took up a new vocation and others were previously clandestine congregations which were now granted legitimacy). By virtue of the Falloux Law, these women needed only a letter of obedience from their Superior to be permitted to teach, rather than the license which was required of secular teachers. Since only about half of the women who took the state licensing examination passed, the Sisters had a great advantage.[20]

In 1853, the Falloux Law was amended to allow women teachers to teach in mixed schools, that is, schools which accepted boys and girls. Though previously this had been thought inappropriate, opinion began to change under the leadership of the church. In 1853, Bishop de Belley explained that a mixed school can be directed by a woman as well as by a man, and "it is clear that a woman teacher, most of all when she comes to a certain age, is much more capable of bringing up young boys than a man can bring up girls." The government supported this point of view. In 1855, the government further amended the law by giving women the exclusive right to direct day-care centers. As a result of these new laws, by 1863, two-thirds of the girls in France attended schools run by Sisters, as did one-fifth of the boys.[21] The secular teachers in boys' schools were more able to resist the dominance of the church for two reasons: first, they frequently acted as assistants to the mayors; and, second, they were relied upon as a political ally of the government during and after the Italian troubles of 1859.

The power of the church in the field of primary education can be judged by the summary in Table 4 prepared by Keller in 1880.[22] The table lists the variety of social services provided by teaching orders which undoubtedly made them more acceptable to village populations. For example, the Little Sisters of the Sick, founded in 1860 in Mauriac, had for their special task, the healing of the sick who were confined to their beds at home. These Sisters, 100 in all, taught approximately 1600 children and took in about 80 orphans to work in *ouvroirs*. The Sisters not only taught and cared for the sick, but they also cared for children whose parents must be temporarily absent; they did housekeeping for the poor, the sick, the

TABLE 4
PERSONS ASSISTED
BY DIOCESE

DIOCESES	CHILDREN INSTRUCTED	Hospitals Clinics	Orphanages Workhouses	Poorhouses Correctional Institutions	Lunatic Asylums Deaf-Dumb Asylums	TOTAL
Agen	1.870	,,	40	,,		40
Aire	450	,,	,,	,,	,,	,,
Aix	7.130	2.500	720	,,	,,	3.220
Ajaccio	,,	,,	,,	,,	,,	,,
Albi	18.565	88	409	100	,,	597
Amiens	31.865	370	345	,,	,,	715
Angers	20.000	,,	,,	3.600	,,	3.600
Angoulême	2.200	600	,,	,,	400	1.000
Annecy	14.474	828	355	,,	2.226	3.409
Arras	10.280	2.519	767	,,	86	3.372
Auch	2.853	20	,,	,,	,,	20
Autun	19.500	1.766	180	,,	,,	1.946
Avignon	3.633	160	7	,,	,,	167
Bayeux	11.138	1.380	484	,,	1.744	3.608
Bayonne	9.252	,,	180	170	,,	350
Beauvais	1.530	156	75	,,	,,	231
Belley	9.115	16	114	,,	,,	130
Besançon	51.595	809	673	481	1.200	3.163
Blois	50	80	265	60	,,	405
Bordeaux	38.405	100	1.020	,,	,,	1.120
Bourges	24.640	5.862	764	,,	,,	6.626
Cahors	11.950	2.605	112	,,	,,	2.717
Cambrai	59.524	3.085	1.197	160	1.610	6.052
Carcassonne	8.570	,,	,,	,,	,,	,,
Chalons	300	,,	,,	,,	,,	,,
Chambéry	6.785	100	160	,,	,,	260
Chartres	21.400	3.800	,,	,,	,,	3.800
Clermont	15.600	,,	320	40	,,	360
Coutances	47.295	315	419	,,	650	1.384
Digne	3.270	50	72	,,	,,	122
Dijon	12.392	991	224	1.333	,,	2.548
Évreux	6.374	540	80	,,	,,	620
Fréjus	3.113	400	,,	,,	,,	400

TABLE 4
PERSONS ASSISTED
BY DIOCESE

DIOCESES	CHILDREN INSTRUCTED	Hospitals Clinics	Orphanages Workhouses	Poorhouses Correctional Institutions	Lunatic Asylums Deaf-Dumb Asylums	TOTAL
Report	475.168	29.140	8.982	5.944	7.916	51.982
Gap	15.611	,,	80	,,	9	89
Grenoble	18.102	71	180	,,	93	344
Langres	15.750	,,	402	,,	,,	402
Laval	33.015	2.920	460	646	,,	4.026
Limoges	7.135	875	790	1.020	,,	2.685
Luçon	74.150	15.050	30	,,	,,	15.080
Lyon	192.571	793	3.050	360	1.505	5.708
Mans (le)	16.00	,,	,,	,,	,,	,,
Marseille	,,	,,	,,	,,	,,	,,
Meaux	2.760	,,	110	,,	,,	110
Mende	1.660	,,	72	,,	,,	72
Montauban	1.930	3	80	150	,,	233
Montpellier	,,	,,	,,	,,	,,	,,
Moulins	,,	,,	,,	,,	,,	,,
Nancy	88.115	325	2.422	,,	,,	2.747
Nantes	17.830	30	300	290	,,	620
Nevers	43.655	7.134	2.412	180	2.880	12.606
Nice	30	27	,,	80	,,	107
Nîmes	3.358	250	380	,,	,,	630
Orléans	3.520	240	,,	,,	,,	240
Pamiers	,,	,,	,,	,,	,,	,,
Paris	576.723	11.673	30.098	1.250	1.886	44.907
Périguex	3.695	567	217	,,	,,	784
Perpignan	3.080	350	,,	,,	,,	350
Poitiers	41.225	100	2.000	,,	,,	2.100
Puy (le)	21.710	460	300	,,	,,	760
Quimper	760	,,	20	,,	,,	20
Reims	10.370	1.400	580	,,	,,	1.980
Rennes	12.200	13.316	80	400	,,	13.796
Rochelle (la)	1.994	,,	175	,,	,,	175
Rodez	43.280	213	531	,,	,,	744
Rouen	70.890	1.875	753	350	,,	2.978
Saint-Brieuc	47.440	1.053	532	200	,,	1.785

TABLE 4
PERSONS ASSISTED
BY DIOCESE

DIOCESES	CHILDREN INSTRUCTED	Hospitals Clinics	Orphanages Workhouses	Poorhouses Correctional Institutions	Lunatic Asylums Deaf-Dumb Asylums	TOTAL
Report	1.843.727	87.865	55.036	10.870	14.289	168.060
Saint-Claude	350	,,	105	25	,,	130
Saint-Dié	80.290	138	222	,,	,,	360
Saint-Flour	2.062	,,	,,	,,	,,	,,
Saint-Jean-de-Maurienne	2.390	80	43	,,	,,	123
Séez	6.720	,,	,,	260	,,	260
Sens	9.800	,,	,,	,,	,,	,,
Soissons	10.470	638	146	,,	,,	784
Tarbes	12.000	,,	,,	,,	,,	,,
Toulouse	,,	,,	,,	,,	,,	,,
Tours	27.084	17.351	1.034	200	,,	18.585
Troyes	9.600	140	230	,,	,,	370
Tulle	1.680	,,	80	,,	,,	80
Valence	38.284	6.972	1.305	,,	,,	8.277
Vannes	75.000	,,	,,	,,	,,	,,
Verdum	2.325	,,	7	160	,,	167
Versailles	6.650	110	155	200	,,	465
Viviers	66.903	835	1.507	,,	72	2.414
Alger, Oran et Constantine	515	,,	305	100	,,	405
TOTAL	2.197.775	114.199	60.225	11.815	14.361	200.600
Religious congregations having their mother house outside of France	11.144	60	40	,,	,,	100
TOTAL GENERAL	2.208.919	114.259	60.265	11.815	14.361	200.700

old. They cut wood, washed and mended laundry, made clothing, cared for animals. In sum, they served all who were incapable of caring for themselves. In 1876 alone, the 100 Little Sisters of the Sick cared for 6,639 people at night; they made 42,000 housekeeping visits and passed 3,304 entire days with families in need.[23]

Gradually, peasants who had resisted sending their children to secular schools, began to send their sons and daughters to schools taught be religious orders. Since regular school attendance and punctuality to a clock schedule was alien to the traditional rhythms of country life, it required the authority of the parish priest to give legitimacy to these new concepts. Since the idea of childhood and education as a phase of life preceding entry into the world of work did not correspond with the experience of peasant families, where the home was the workplace and the child was familiar with the family's labor from his earliest days, the peasants had to be given good reasons to send their children to school. Having Sisters in the community who not only taught, but also provided care for the sick and the elderly as well as aid for the needy, were excellent reasons.

Thus, the reflowering of church authority over primary education was encouraged by the state as a result of the fear brought on by the Revolution of 1848, while it simultaneously filled the need of the Church for a secure place in an increasingly secularized world. The success of the church in primary education was due to its ability to coax the peasants into the modern world. Ironically, it was the church that had both the authority and the personnel to accomplish the secular goals set forth by Guizot. In addition to its enormous influence through the teaching orders, the church also trained many secular teachers in religious normal schools, while even the secular normal schools for girls had a distinctly religious flavor.

The daily program of young women who attended the secular Ecole Normale d'Institutrices at Saint-Egrève (near Grenoble) from 1857 to 1872 was a good example of the strong influence of the cloisters on a secular institution. Under the rules of the establishment were listed:

Religious duties: Prayer each day in the chapel, morning and night. Prayer for the return to classes also takes place in the chapel, morning, 2:00 P.M., and evening. Before and after meals a teacher says the benediction and grace in a loud voice. When one awakes and is still in bed, a teacher will recite in a loud voice the morning prayer. The rosary is said in the dormitories when going to sleep at night. One recites it while doing homework, when possible. It is also said on Sunday, after morning prayer, after a reading, preferably an "imitation of Jesus Christ" . . . Thursday after mass the curé teaches the catechism. It is required that one take the sacraments every month.[24]

The quarter century following the uprisings of 1848 was characterized by growing religious influence over primary education of the poor. As we have seen, nuns and priests were in a unique position to influence peasant parents to send their children to school. The numbers of clerical teachers grew, the education of secular teachers was influenced by the religious domination of many normal schools, and the books used in schools were frequently sent to religious authorities for endorsement.

CHAPTER FOUR

The Contribution of Zulma Carraud

Two of the books endorsed by the church in the 1850s were written by Zulma Carraud: *La Petite Jeanne ou le devoir* in 1853 and *Maurice ou le travail* in 1855. Together these two books sold nearly one million copies by 1900 and probably influenced millions of children. Excerpts from both of these volumes follow in Part II.

Zulma Carraud entered the world of rural schools and peasant children with a very different background from that of her pupils and readers. She was born on March 24, 1796, in Issoudon. Her father, Rémi Tourangin, was a man of enlightened ideas who prospered under the revolutionary and Napoleonic regimes. Zulma was sent to a boarding school for young ladies where she met Laure de Balzac, who remained a lifelong companion. Through Laure, Zulma met Honoré de Balzac; he became a close friend until his death in 1850.[1]

Zulma's early education probably included the typical subjects taught in schools for upper-middle-class girls: "lecture élémentaire, lecture perfectionée, écriture, grammaire, arithmétique, système métrique, histoire sainte, histoire de France, histoire ancienne, histoire moderne, cosmographie, géographie, littérature, physique et chimie, histoire naturelle."[2] In 1816 she married François Michel Carraud, a second cousin, fifteen years her senior, an artillery captain and former polytechnic student; they lived in Saint-Cyr where M. Carraud was the director of studies at the Royal Military Academy from 1818 to 1831. There, Zulma frequently entertained

Balzac and the other literary members of the community. It is through the correspondence between Zulma Carraud and Honoré de Balzac that we have some information about her ideas with regard to children and teaching.[3]

In her mid-thirties, Zulma wrote to Honoré from a new home in Angoulême that she was very depressed because of lack of stimulation of friends, but:

"Happily, I have a reason for living—my son! Oh you who know so much, you can't imagine what a son means to his mother: his mother, charged with his future; helping him deal with "real" life while keeping in mind the "ideal" life during moments of respite; committed to the formation of a true man's heart. . .; creating a logical mind without undoing his imagination.[4]

Zulma's consuming involvement with the education of her two sons, Ivan and Yorick, gradually convinced her that her special interest was education.

You know that my hobby is education. I have studied this subject in depth, as much as a woman can, and I have come to the conclusion that the early years of life are the most important as far as education is concerned.[5]

Her interest in education was given a chance to express itself outside of her immediate family several years later when the Carrauds suffered financial reverses and, to cut expenses, moved to Nohant to live with Zulma's brother. There, she was caught up in the spirit of the times which encouraged women with Zulma's background to react maternally to the social upheaval of 1848. Whether motivated by genuine desire to help the poor or by fear of revolution, the result was the same: middle-class women saw themselves as spreading their maternal wings to care for the poor by socializing their children to "better" ways. This feeling was synthesized in a petition signed by 106 ladies demanding that the mayor of Paris open crèches, day-care centers, school workshops, and refuges in poor neighborhoods. They argued: "The virtues and devotions of one class must conquer the vice and unhappiness of the other." [6]

It was thus in the small village of Nohant, department of the

9. Zulma Carraud

Cher, that Zulma Carraud began teaching (c. 1850). Carraud had arrived in Nohant at a propitious moment. The student population of the Cher was growing, but the number of *instituteurs* had been cut back because of their involvement in politics. The schools in the Cher were not unlike those described in the preceding chapters: There were 184 boys' public schools and 51 girls' public schools; 23

boys' private schools and 58 girls' private schools. Most of the schools (301 of them) had adopted the simultaneous method of education, but according to the school inspector, only 172 of them used good books in the classroom. Apparently some others were open to change because the inspector noted that 91 teachers employed some good books, while 53 used only bad books.[7]

Perhaps Zulma concurred with the school inspector, that much was still to be done in the area of appropriate school books for rural girls and boys. Perhaps she was also influenced by her long friendship with Balzac. What is certain is that she began to write almost immediately after beginning her teaching career. Her first book, *La Petite Jeanne ou le devoir* was published two years later. As her original contract with Louis Hachette shows, the book was destined from the beginning to be a reader for rural girls' schools and Hachette was confident that sales would be good — the first print run was for 5,000 copies.[8]

The success of *La Petite Jeanne* was due to the fact that it filled the great need for books designed to appeal to rural girls and their teachers. A year later Carraud published *Maurice ou le travail* to fill the same need for boys' schools in the countryside. Sales records for the various editions: littérature populaire (popular edition), Bibliothèque Rose (illustrated), papier fin (luxury edition) of both books were kept by Hachette for 1864-1920. During these years *Jeanne* sold 434,548 copies and *Maurice* sold 428,498, as outlined in Table 5. These large numbers are explained in part by the fact that both books were adopted as readers in many French departments. The *Liste Scolaire* of 1889 shows *Maurice* required in 23 departments and *Jeanne* in 21 departments.[9]

Like many of the earlier writers discussed above, Carraud sought to inculcate values while teaching her students to read. These values, however, were specifically aimed at peasant children and at their parents as well. Carraud was the first children's writer of importance to create main characters who were neither noble, bourgeois, nor working class. Jeanne and Maurice were children whose roots were in the village and they were set up by Carraud as role models for all peasant children. The Minister of Public Instruction and Beaux-Arts and the Archbishop of Paris both, endorsed Carraud's books as reading of high moral value.[10]

Table 5. Sale of Carraud's Jeanne and Maurice, 1864-1920

JEANNE

YEARS	Popular Edition	Bibliothèque Rose	Luxury Edition
1864-1873	173,699	20,764	830
1874-1883	178,877	14,153	
1884-1893	23,712	6,748	
1894-1903	5,157	4,222	
1904-1913		4,505	
1914-1920		1848	

MAURICE

YEARS	Popular Edition	Bibliothèque Rose	Luxury Edition
1864-1873	221,100		1,211
1874-1883	190,609		
1884-1893	12,109		
1894-1903	2,681		
1904-1913	664		
1914-1920	124		

In *La Petite Jeanne* there are four main themes: first, women, as part of their religious heritage, have duties to others; second, deferential personal relationships are preferable to market (impersonal) relationships; third, a new outlook should be adopted in limited areas, notably health and basic education; fourth, a preference for rural life and maintenance of most traditions is strong.

The main characters in the book are all women: Mère Nannette is a sixty-year-old childless widow who worked very hard, lived frugally, and managed to own her home and garden. Catherine is a young and very frail widow who is impoverished after helping her husband through a long illness; Mme. Dumont is a wealthy and generous neighbor who agrees to help raise Jeanne (Catherine's daughter) because of the latter's good character; Isaure is Mme. Dumont's daughter, Jeanne's age, who teaches Jeanne many skills; Maîtresse Tixier is the kind wife of the farmer where Jeanne is in service; Solange is Tixier's daughter who is taught by Jeanne how to improve her wanton ways; Nannette is Jeanne's daughter who learns from her mother how to be just like her.

The lives of these characters are governed by duties, personal relationships, limited acceptance of new ways and preferences for country living and traditions. The plot follows the life of Jeanne whom we meet first as a young girl walking down a country road with her mother, Catherine. The two women approached the door of Mère Nannette, begging their bread. After listening to Catherine's sad tale, Mère Nannette offered the two strangers permanent shelter.

The following day when Jeanne and her mother were returning home from an afternoon of begging, Jeanne spied a gold bracelet lying in the grass. She was delighted by its beauty and wished to keep it, but Catherine insisted that it was her duty to search out the rightful owner. Mère Nannette told them that it could only belong to Mme. Dumont and the next day they went to the château to return the bracelet. When Catherine was offered a reward by the overjoyed Mme. Dumont she replied: "O! Merci Madame; je n'ai fait que mon devoir en vous rendant ce qui vous appartient: je ne dois pas en être récompensée" ("Oh! Thank you Madame; I have only done my duty in returning what belongs to you; I must not be rewarded"). But, Madame Dumont insisted on giving her fifteen francs plus a small weekly allowance to Jeanne.

Gradually, a close personal relationship developed between the Dumonts and Jeanne, who visited them weekly to pick up her allowance. Isaure taught Jeanne how to read and write and do some simple arithmetic. She also instructed her in knitting. Jeanne was a devoted pupil and pleased Isaure and Mme. Dumont.

After Catherine's death, when Jeanne was only eight years old, Mère Nannette became a mother to the orphaned girl. She counseled her against ever leaving the countryside. Though one can earn more in the city, she explained to Jeanne that one spends more also, "et les jeunes filles y ont bien du désagrément" ("and the young girls find it very unpleasant there"). When Mère Nannette died, Jeanne was eighteen. She soon followed the old women's advice of seeking a job in the countryside.

Jeanne went into service at Grand Bail, a neighboring farm where her employer, Maître Tixier and his wife, were very pleased with her dutiful behavior, expressed in terms of very hard work; her personal ties to her employers and their children, especially her devotion to Solange; her cleanliness and ability to read aloud to the family; and her adherence to traditional respect for her masters.

At her new home Jeanne met Grand Louis, the best laborer at Grand Bail. On one occasion Jeanne secretly mended Louis' clothes because she wished to do a service for this good worker and for her master. When Louis learned who had fixed his clothes he wanted to pay her for her work, but Jeanne saw the work as her duty and wished only friendship in return.

Two years later Grand Louis asked Jeanne to marry him; Jeanne agreed, but her loyalty to her employers forced her to ask him to wait. She explained that her mistress was ailing and was not able to do any work; Solange, the oldest daughter, was Jeanne's age and would probably marry soon and leave home; Josephine, the next daughter was only seventeen and, in Jeanne's view, much too young to take over running the household. Jeanne concluded: "I cannot leave my masters, for I love them so very much." Grand Louis agreed to wait for Jeanne.

In chapter three, "Jeanne épouse et mère," Carraud instructed her readers about limited acceptance of new ideas. Carraud praised Jeanne for planning to build a house that was different from those of her neighbors. Jeanne consulted Mme. Isaure to get advice about building a house that would not be damp, dark, and dirty. She was able to get Mme. Isaure to draw up plans from which Grand Louis worked. The building took longer and cost a little more than most peasant homes, but Carraud implied that it was worth the expense.

Jeanne's new ways were most developed with regard to child care. Unlike her neighbors, Jeanne made certain that her children were combed and washed. Her neighbors chided her for putting on bourgeois airs. Jeanne replied that being a peasant was no reason for children to be dirty. When the women asked her how she kept her children's clothing looking new, Jeanne explained how she would fold them carefully every night. In addition, she did not permit her children to eat all day long and made a point of covering them with bibs at mealtimes.

Thus, for women, the new behavior which was advocated—planning, cleanliness, health care—involved women's role as child-rearer. As Patricia Branca pointed out in her study of Victorian women, this led to ambiguous messages for women who were urged to be independent enough to plan and who were thought to be capable enough to care for health needs, but at the same time remained entirely at the disposal of the children for whom they were caring.[11] Jeanne served her children with the same type of selflessness she expressed when caring for Mère Nannette and Maîtresse Tixier.

Jeanne's devotion to others was an important aspect of the close mother-daughter relationship that grew between Jeanne and her daughter, Nannette. Nannette understood Jeanne and resembled her very much. "Nannette had such a happy temperament that everyone loved her, just as everyone had loved her mother when she was a young girl." Nannette was the only one who could help her mother with Paul, her bad-tempered brother. Her patient care made him less violent.

Like her mother before her, Nannette developed close personal ties with the Dumonts when she went to work for them in the chapter, "Jeanne Veuve." After several months, Solange came to Jeanne and asked permission for her son, Jean, to marry Nannette. Jean would come to live with Jeanne and his new bride and would work their land. Jeanne was delighted with the idea and went to ask Nannette's opinion. Nannette said she wanted to marry, but was afraid to offend Mme. Isaure by leaving so soon. When consulted, Mme. Isaure was surprised that Jeanne didn't wish her daughter to marry a city dweller. Nannette explained, "Madame, I know of only two homes in which I could ever live: yours and that of my mother. If I had not found a man who wished to live with her I would never leave your service." Thus, despite the fact that Nannette had been brought up in a cleaner, more orderly, and more instructed manner than her neighbors, she would not give up her rural ties to embark on a new way of life.

Maurice ou le travail is also concerned with four main themes: first, the husband becomes the sole source of well-being for his family, though he recognizes the need for a wife to care for his home and children; second, order, discipline, work, perseverance, and patience lead to success; third, there is acceptance of the idea of progress and planning for the future; fourth, the tradition of respect for elders and settling in the village of your birth are recommended.

The main characters are Jérôme, Maurice's father and a good

worker; Grand'Biche, a poor old spinster who became a substitute mother for Maurice; M. Rémi, Maurice's teacher who helps him to progress; and the curé, who reminds Maurice of his duties.

The story follows the life of Maurice whom we first meet as a lonely, four-year-old boy whose mother has died. His father was a wheelwright and often was forced to work away from home. Jérôme worried about Maurice and asked Grand'Biche to come and live in his house to care for Maurice and do the household chores.

Grand'Biche kept the house orderly, prepared food well and economically, and taught Maurice to keep clean and neat. When Maurice was six, Jérôme wanted him to begin his schooling. Grand'Biche saw no need for it, but Jérôme believed in progress and in planning for his son's future: "It is important that my son do better than me. Ignorant people are suspicious of everyone and always believe that others are out to trick them; such thoughts spoil one's heart and soul." Maurice learned, both at home and at school, to love order and work.

When Maurice was only eight, Jérôme broke his leg and became paralyzed for life; he was never able to work again. Maurice tried to help his family by doing odd jobs for the village blacksmith and herding cattle to a nearby village. When Grand'Biche protested that Maurice was too young to take such a job, Jérôme explained that it was necessary for him to become accustomed to fatigue early in life so that he might learn to earn his living.

Maurice did his work with great care and was well appreciated by his employer. When he came home he signed on as an apprentice to the village blacksmith. He continued his studies with M. Rémi after work each day. When M. Rémi urged Jérôme to send his son to an advanced school for arts and sciences, the curé advised that Maurice remain at home to study while continuing his apprenticeship and consoling his ailing father. Maurice remained at home, choosing to fulfill filial obligations at the expense of personal growth. He worked hard and was a source of comfort to his father.

Jérôme died when Maurice was fifteen. For the next three years Maurice continued to work as an apprentice blacksmith. He followed his tutor's advice: "Le travail est après la prière le plus grand remède aux peines de cette vie" ("After prayer, work is the best remedy for life's pains"). Then Maurice decided to go on the *Tour de France* (a traditional visit to the major artisan centers) to improve his skills. Though Grand'Biche was desolate, Maurice explained that provincialism bred ignorance and that he would return home a better worker. In this way, Carraud balanced the tug between tradition and change. Maurice would advance beyond his father's level, but not reach too high.

Maurice's first stop was in Bourges, where he learned to profit from the advice and company of older workers. He learned the secret of good work—perseverance at one's task. After several months, he left for Paris, where he quickly fell in with a group of wanton boys and wound up in jail following a brawl. This bad experience taught Maurice the dangers of bad friends and he quickly resumed the straight and narrow. He became the most valued employee of M. Blanchard, a smith. He was orderly and careful. He helped the younger boys to learn their jobs. By the time he left Paris for home and the draft, the Blanchards had come to think of him as a second son.

His reunion with Grand'Biche was warm, but brief. By the time he returned from his military service, where he excelled, she was dead. Maurice found a job with a blacksmith in a neighboring village and shortly thereafter married his employer's daughter. Maurice continued to work in his father-in-law's shop for a few years and then packed up his wife and two young children and went home to his own village to start a workshop of his own.

In the next few years Maurice worked harder than ever to get himself established as the best blacksmith in the vicinity. With patience and diligence he built his business, his shop, and later his house. When his wife worried about their lack of economic security, Maurice told her, "Have faith in me." His habit of working when troubled stood him in good stead and gradually his business prospered.

Maurice instructed his son, Charles, in the business and was pleased to see him develop into a good worker. He also took on apprentices and treated them as sons, teaching them good work habits as well as skills. At the same time, Maurice encountered a childhood friend, Frisé, who had despaired of becoming a responsible citizen and had gone on the dole. Maurice convinced him that it was shameful to take charity unless he was sick. He showed Frisé how to economize and how to put order into his life. Maurice believed that people had a free choice to follow good or bad instincts and that one had only one's self to blame for making the wrong choices.

One day, M. Berthaud, one of Maurice's wealthy clients asked him why a well-educated and intelligent person, such as he chose to live in this small town. He seemed to think that Maurice was necessarily bored with the lack of stimulating neighbors and distractions. Maurice, however, stated that he was constantly learning things from his neighbors, things of which he was quite ignorant. He even learned from the women who visited his home in the evening. Thus, Maurice remained faithful to his background, continued a good relationship with his father-in-law, his teacher, and his priest, while he developed his business.

Charles went off to the army, despite his mother's fears, and like his father learned much about the country and different methods of cultivation and industry. When he returned he married Clementine, a second cousin, and was given a house, adjoining that of his parents, as a wedding present. But, Charles lamented to Maurice that he would never be able to become the sole source of his family's well-being, as Maurice had been. Maurice told him that he had an equally important task, that of conserving wealth.

Gradually, Charles began to take over more and more of the business and Maurice had more time for other things. He was appointed assistant mayor of the village and worked on improving roads, squares, and buildings. He showed the villagers how to put their spare moments to good use for the community, as he had done for his business.

The role models Carraud worked out in her first two books, *La Petite Jeanne* and *Maurice* were developed, but not changed, in several other children's books which she wrote in the next few years: *Historiettes à l'usage des jeunes enfants qui commencent à savoir lire* (1835), *Historiettes à l'usage des jeunes enfants de quatre à huit ans* (1864), *Les Métamorphoses d'une goutte d'eau* (1864), *Une Servante d'autrefois* (1866), *Le livre des jeunes filles, simple correspondance* (1868). *Les Goûters de la grand-mère* (1868), and *Les Veillées de Maître Patrigeon* (1868). All the books were published by Hachette in the years indicated and were reprinted several times, in some cases reedited.[12] Some were translated into Italian, others into Spanish, and a request came from the United States for the rights to translate *La Petite Jeanne* into English. Zulma Carraud died in 1889 at the age of 94, having influenced millions of children with her words.[13]

PART TWO

Selections from Zulma Carraud's Children's Books: La Petite Jeanne ou le devoir and Maurice ou le travail

The following selections have been edited and translated to highlight the adult roles French children were taught in La Petite Jeanne *and* Maurice. *Each book has been divided into four sections: I. Childhood, II. Young Adulthood, III. Family, IV. Old Age. The sections are juxtaposed to focus on the distinct roles prescribed for men and women. Each section is prefaced by a short introduction.*

CHAPTER FIVE

Childhood

The families in which Jeanne and Maurice grew up did not have the ideal structure advocated by the middle-class leaders of the nineteenth century. Jeanne's family consisted of her mother, Catherine, and Mère Nannette, an old woman who took in the poor widow and her daughter. Likewise, Maurice lived with his widower father, Jérôme, and Grand'Biche, an old woman who acted as a substitute mother for the boy. Though both children did not experience the nuclear family structure recommended by the bourgeoisie, their parents taught them middle-class values—cleanliness, punctuality, perseverance, saving, and delayed rewards. In this way Carraud cleverly sketched for her rural readers a family structure that would be familiar to them while teaching values they did not yet accept.

Catherine and Jérôme were valuable to the stories because they represented a transition between old and new values. They both regarded their way of life as "not good enough" for their children, a new concept in the nineteenth century. Catherine and Jérôme supported the idea of marriage as a family partnership with specialized roles for each member: men provided economic support and women provided moral guidance. Since both of them lost spouses early in their family lives, they were forced to seek substitute arrangements, but the message of specialized roles was impressed on Jeanne and Maurice.

Jeanne and Maurice learned many values and some skills from their parents, but they also learned from outside influences. The priest was important in both stories, providing guidance at crucial moments. Jeanne learned skills—reading, writing, arithmetic and knitting from the Dumont family (wealthy land owners), while Maurice learned similar skills from M. Rémi, his teacher. In these chapters on childhood we begin to see the emergence of two different trends: For Jeanne, self-esteem developed from being loved and accepted by others—Mère Nannette, Mme. Dumont, the priest; while Maurice began to value himself for visible achievements—his house, his workshop, his family's comfortable position.

Childhood ended precipitously for both children when their respective families collapsed due to the death of Jérôme in Maurice's case and Mère Nannette in Jeanne's. The young adults were left disoriented but continued to acquire values and skills in a new approved structure: for Jeanne, service on a neighboring farm; for Maurice, the *Tour de France*.

Jeanne's Childhood

(Mère Nannette was a sixty-year-old, childless widow. She owned a small home and a garden. She was hard-working, self-sufficient.)

One morning, when Mère Nannette was knitting in front of her door, she saw a young woman approaching. The woman held a little girl of seven or eight years of age by the hand, and asked for a piece of bread. The woman was very pale and looked sick, so Mère Nannette called her into the house and made her sit down. She lit her fire again, warmed up what was left of her soup, which she had planned to eat at supper, and gave it to the two beggars. The child ate with such appetite that Mère Nannette could clearly see that the little girl did not often have enough to eat.

(Catherine explained to Mère Nannette that she was recently widowed. Her husband had been ill for a long time and had left Catherine destitute. Mère Nannette offered Catherine shelter.)

When the mother and daughter had had some rest, they went on their way to ask for bread in the village and said they would be back at night. Since it was the season for plums and currants, Mère Nannette went to pick some in her garden and put them in Jeanne's bag so that she could refresh herself when she got too warm.

When they were crossing the road on their way back to Mère Nannette's

10. Mère Nannette

house after finishing their rounds, little Jeanne saw something glittering in the sun; she ran to pick it up and brought it promptly to her mother.

"Look, mother, what a nice necklace I found! I'll put it on next Sunday."

"My little girl, this jewelry is to be worn on the wrist. It is a bracelet. It does not belong to us, and we cannot keep it."

"What if nobody asks for it?"

"It should not prevent us from looking for the person to whom the bracelet belongs. We'll ask about it all around the village."

"And if it belongs to no one?"

"Then, we'll guard it with care. Eventually, somebody will come to ask for it."

11. Catherine and Jeanne

When they returned to Mère Nannette, they showed her what they had found, and asked if she knew who could have lost such beautiful jewelry. "It could be no one but Mme. Dumont. In this area only she wears such things. She lives in the neighborhood, behind the beautiful trees that you can easily see from here. You should take it back to her at once if you are not too tired. I'm sure she's worried about it."

"I'm too weary to walk now, but tomorrow morning I'll go to see the lady with Jeanne, and I'll give her back what belongs to her. Since we were given a lot today and I am so tired, I will rest tomorrow all day, to be able to go to my village on Saturday to ask Maître Guillaume to move my bed here."

The next morning, Catherine combed Jeanne's long black hair more carefully than she usually did. She washed her face and hands, dressed her in her neatest clothes, and they went off to see Mme. Dumont. They stopped at the railing which opened into a beautiful garden, but, since there was nobody there, Catherine followed the wall and saw a big door leading into the yard. The door was open. A servant saw her and brought her a piece of bread and a penny.

"Thank you, mademoiselle," said Catherine, "but I'd like to talk to your mistress."

"My poor woman, you cannot see her at this hour."

"Well then, can you ask her if she lost this thing which I found yesterday in the big road?" She showed her the jewelry wrapped in a white rag.

"That's it! The bracelet that Madame lost yesterday when she went for a walk with the children! She will be happy to have it back, for we were looking for it until nightfall. I'll take it to her while you wait, my good woman. Sit down on the bench. And you, little one, come with me. You'll give the bracelet to the lady yourself."

The maid took Jeanne by the hand and let her into the house. They went up the grand staircase and crossed a room filled with beautiful furniture. Jeanne opened her eyes very wide, for she had never seen anything like this. They came into another room with two beds , all white.

Mme. Dumont was busy combing her little girl's hair. The girl was the same age as Jeanne: "Oh, mother, look what a pretty little girl!"

Mme. Dumont raised her eyes, and the servant told her, "This child found Madame's bracelet and is bringing it back. Now, little one, go ahead. The lady is kind, don't be afraid.

Jeanne let the maid lead her, her head hanging down, not daring even to raise her eyes.

The lady told her, "You do not realize what pleasure you give me, my child, bringing back my bracelet. Now tell me, who are you?"

Since Jeanne remained silent, the servant answered for her. "Madame, her mother is downstairs at the door. She's a poor woman who begs her bread."

"I'll go down to see her as soon as I fix Isaure's hair."

Then Mme. Dumont went down, followed by Isaure and the maid, who still held Jeanne by the hand. When she arrived at the bottom of the staircase she called Catherine, and, seeing her pallor, told her to sit down.

"I wonder, where did you find my bracelet?"

"Madame, it was Jeanne, my little daughter, who saw it glistening in the sun and picked it up beside the ditch on the road."

"Thank you for bringing it back, and here are fifteen francs to reward your honesty."

"Oh, thank you Madame! I only did my duty bringing back what belongs to you. I don't have to be rewarded."

"Well then, since you gave me a great pleasure, I also want to do something good for you, so take the money anyway!"

"God bless you, Madame, for being so good to us! . . . "

"Catherine, you will send your daughter here every Friday, and I'll give her a coin of fifty centimes."

"May God reward you, Madame."

Then Catherine, taking her daughter by the hand, went out to return to Mère Nannette's.

On coming in, she showed her the three five-franc coins she was given. "Take this, Mère Nannette. It will help you a little, for it is not fair that you give me shelter for nothing when I can give you something."

"You should well know, Catherine, that I don't want to take anything for helping you. It's no big trouble for me to have you in my house, which is big enough for both of us, and my fireplace can boil your pot at the same time with mine, but give me your money and I'll keep it for you so that you can buy what you'll need."

(Catherine returned to her village to pick up her belongings.)

The next day, as she woke up, little Jeanne called to her mother, then, remembering she was not there, she got up, dressed herself and asked Mère Nannette to wash her and to comb her hair, as Catherine always did. Then she knelt down and said her prayer.

"What prayers do you know?" asked Mère Nannette.

"I know *Our Father* and *I welcome you, Marie.*"

"Say them aloud."

Jeanne recited them without missing one word. When she finished, she remained on her knees and Mère Nannette asked her, "What else are you saying there?"

"I'm asking the good Lord to have pity on us, and to bless those who help us. Your name comes first, then that of Mme. Dumont. Mother told me yesterday to say it this way."

The bells chimed for the Mass and Mère Nannette put on nice clothes. She looked at little Jeanne, and seeing that her shawl was all torn, she gave her one of her own. After that they left for the church, each of them carrying a chair. During the mass Jeanne kept the rosary which Mère Nannette gave to her and said her prayers. She never turned her head to see who was coming in or going out. She knelt down when everybody else did and stood up with the others.

(Catherine returned to Mère Nannette and Jeanne. The next day . . .)

Catherine took her daughter by the hand and gave her the bag. They made their rounds of the town and of the small farms around. Passing by the priest's door, they stopped there and he called them in. "My good woman," he said to Catherine, "why don't you place your child at some farmer's who would send her into the fields to watch cattle? She would be happier there than she is with you, and she won't learn to beg. Be careful! You'll make a vagabond out of her."

"Father, I thought about it a long time ago and I tell you, it's a great grief for me to see her begging at doors. There are days when she doesn't have the heart to beg, but I'm so weak and ill; I won't be able to go out in the winter."

"Why so?"

"Because doctors forbade me to go out. They say that my lungs are infected. I cough a lot and I cannot work. If Jeanne does not bring bread for me, I'll starve to death! But you should not worry, Father, I'll place her with decent people as soon as I can. It's too much grief for me to be a beggar at my age and to wish my daughter to do the same!"

"You are right, my good woman. We'll see quite soon what we can do for you. Meanwhile, come here every Sunday to get your twenty-five centimes."

"Thank you very much, Father. With those twenty-five centimes, and the other fifty that Mme. Dumont gives me, we'll be able to buy some clothes, for I'm ashamed of our rags."

The next Friday when Jeanne awoke, she said to her mother, "Today we have to go to see the lady about our fifty centimes. We'll go, mother, won't we?"

"My girl, you'll go there alone, for I have to help Mère Nannette with the laundry, and you'll go there in the morning so that when you come back you'll take the goslings and the goat to the fields."

"Mother, I won't ever dare go into that beautiful house alone."

"Why not, my Jeanne? The lady is so kind that you don't have to be afraid to talk to her. I'll dress you as neatly as I can. Will you be able to find the house?"

"Oh yes! I'll follow the creek up to the mill and I'll be right there."

As she left, Jeanne took a stick with her to defend herself from any wild dogs she might meet. When she came to the garden railing, she saw M. and Mme. Dumont eating lunch with their children under the arbor of honeysuckle. Isaure, the little girl with bond hair, saw Jeanne first. "Mother, here is the pretty little girl who brought back the bracelet!" She got up to open the gate, but her brother, August, who was already thirteen, ran faster than she did and let Jeanne in.

"You came to get your fifty centimes?" asked Isaure, who was not any bigger than Jeanne. Then with her mother's permission, she took a huge piece of a plum tart that was on the table, and gave it to Jeanne. "Eat my little one; it's good." Jeanne took the tart but didn't eat it. "Are you not hungry?"

"I am, miss, I did not have my breakfast yet."

"Maybe you don't like the tart?"

"I don't know, I never ate one; but it smells so good! I believe it is even better than plain cake.

"Why then don't you eat it?"

Jeanne did not answer. Then Mme. Dumont, too, asked Jeanne why she didn't touch her piece of the tart. She answered, lowering her head, "Because I'd like to take it to my mother and Mère Nannette to eat as a snack."

"My child, there's nothing wrong with that, on the contrary, you do well when you share the good things you have with Mère Nannette who helps you in your great distress; but here is another little piece and you are going to eat it here, in front of me."

Several days later, Isaure said, "Mother, what if we go to see little Jeanne and that kind Mère Nannette?"

"Very well," said Mme. Dumont. So, she started on her way with her two daughters and a son. When they approached the town they asked a man who was digging in his garden at the side of the road, where Mère Nannette's house was; he showed them a big walnut tree that stood at a distance, in front of the door. When they entered, they found Catherine, the widow, churning butter. Mme. Dumont asked her where her daughter was.

"She's in bed, Madame."

"Is she sick?" asked Isaure promptly and turned to the bed where one could see Jeanne's pretty face on the bolster.

"Thank God, no, my dear Mademoiselle, but I've washed her clothes this morning and, since she has no others, she has to stay in bed while they dry out."

"And where is Mère Nannette?"

"She is watching her animals, but she'll be back soon. Madame, would you like to sit down and wait for her; you'll relax. We have only three chairs, but the young master can sit on the trunk."

As soon as she came in, Mme. Dumont saw at first sight that the house and the furniture were very clean; so she sat down without any fear.

While her mother was talking, Isaure climbed onto the chair at Jeanne's bedside and spoke to her. "You must be bored in bed, aren't you, little Jeanne?"

"Yes, Mademoiselle. I would rather get up and watch Mère Nannette's goslings, but my mother had to wash my clothes; she says it is bad enough to be poor and that we should not disgust those whose comfort us."

"So you go every day to ask for bread?"

"Oh, no, Mademoiselle. When we are given enough, we stay at home as long as we have some. It's so painful to beg at doors."

"Do they always give when you ask for something."

"Mademoiselle, I do not ask; I stay at the door until they give me something. Quite often there is nobody in the house during the harvest time or at hay making. On those days I don't get much."

"And if you don't get anything?"

"We go to bed without supper; it happened to us more than once before we met Mère Nannette, but she doesn't want us to suffer from hunger, and when we have no bread, she lends us some."

"Do you sometimes go to play with other little girls of the town in the church square?"

"Oh, Mademoiselle, they would not want me!"

"Really! Why so?"

"Because I beg for my living."

"You know, that is ugly if they behave like that!"

Mère Nannette came back, and Mme. Dumont generously praised the poor widow and her child.

(Isaure wished to give Jeanne one of her extra dresses, but Mme. Dumont suggested that Isaure make her a useful dress instead. Sophie, Isaure, and the rest of the family took part in contributing to a new outfit for Jeanne. Jeanne was delighted with her new clothes, which she saved for church and her visits to the Dumonts.)

On the eve of market day, Jeanne, while watching the goslings, noticed beautiful flowers in the hedge of a large meadow and on the side of the creek that ran through the woods. She decided to make bouquets. She mixed them with sprigs of all kinds of meadow herbs, and when they were ready, she put them in a thick clump of sod for the night. Then she went to Mère Nannette and asked her if she could go with her when she went to town so that she could sell her bouquets. Mère Nannette agreed, and the next day Catherine dressed Jeanne in her beautiful clothes. The child found her flowers as fresh as if she just picked them.

No sooner had Mère Nannette arrived at the market place, when everybody asked her where she found such a pretty little girl. "She's a poor child who begs her bread," she answered.

"She's well dressed for a beggar!"

"That's because charitable ladies took pity on her and dressed her like that."

While looking at little Jeanne they were looking at her bouquets, and bargained for them with her. "Pay me as much as you like. It is for my mother who is ill."

They gave her ten centimes for her flowers. Some ladies who were shopping even gave her fifteen or twenty, for they found her so nice. She sold all her bouquets and brought one franc to her mother. After that, every time when the weather was fine, she made her bouquets in order to sell them. She was not always paid as much for them, but she liked it better than begging at doors.

(Isaure taught Jeanne to knit.)

"Are your hands clean?" Mme. Dumont asked her.

"Yes, Madame, I've rubbed them in the bran that Mère Nannette put up to boil for her goslings. Mother uses a very sharp little chip of wood to clean my nails."

"So, your mother is very clean, isn't she?"

"Yes, Madame; every morning she combs her hair in the shed, and mine too, and when she went to beg for bread with me, we always used to stop at the creek to wash our feet."

"Do you usually say your prayers, little Jeanne?"

"Oh yes, Madame. I say them every night and every morning. In fine weather we say them outside, and when we pass by a church, we always go in to pray to Child Jesus."

"And what do you ask from Child Jesus?"

"I ask him to let me grow up big and strong to earn my living, so that I won't have to beg from those who owe me nothing."

"So, you'll be quite happy when you go to work?"

"Oh yes, Madame, that is certain."

"And what will you do with the money that you will earn when you grow up?"

"I'll give bread and a dress to mother, and then I will also give something to Mère Nannette who is so charitable to us."

"But she doesn't seem to lack for anything, your Mère Nannette."

"Madame, she is not rich, and if she did not save all the time, she would hardly be able to make ends meet."

In two weeks Jeanne could knit well enough to make a stocking. Sophie started one for her, and Jeanne was very happy to show her mother and Mère Nannette how she worked. When she watched the geese and the two ducklings, she always had the stocking in her hands; she did not leave it even when she went to the door. People who saw her so hard at work often gave her something with her bread, such as vegetables to make soup, and when they were making flat cakes in the farms it was quite rare if one did not save little Jeanne a share.

(Sophie and Isaure taught Jeanne to read and do arithmetic. They continued to practice knitting. One afternoon when Jeanne failed to come to her lessons, the sisters were very concerned. Jeanne was always prompt. Sophie and Isaure went with their mother to Mère Nannette's house and learned that Catherine was dying. Mère Nannette went to take care of Jeanne who was only eight years old. Catherine died. Mme. Dumont paid fifteen francs for the burial.)

"Mère Nannette, you should continue to send Jeanne to our house. My daughters will teach her how to write and do all kinds of needle work. I take it upon myself to provide for her living, so you won't have to spend anything for her."

Jeanne continued to go to Mme. Dumont's where she soon learned everything they had to teach her. The two young ladies, seeing her so good natured and hard-working, became more and more attached to her. The priest, who always saw her so quiet in church, gave her beautiful pictures from time to time. When she could read well he presented her with a little prayer-book, which made her feel happy.

At the age of twelve, she could read and write fairly well; she could do all kinds of needlework very neatly. Mère Nannette taught her to spin thread, and her thread was already finer than that of many weavers in the town, because she paid a lot of attention to what she did.

(Jeanne, who was very pious, and Isaure made their first communion together.)

After her first communion, Jeanne did not stop going to Mme. Dumont's. Every Sunday, they taught her to write, read, and count, so that she would not forget what she already knew.

On wash days she helped to soap the linen, to put it into the washing-blue, to stretch and to fold it; she ironed sheets and towels and mended what was torn. Eventually, she even learned how to iron fine linen. When someone was invited for dinner, Jeanne helped the cook in the kitchen and the servant who set the table. That's how she learned a little bit of service. They always paid her for the days when she worked at the mansion. Since she could sew very well, Mère Nannette, who knew many people in the town, used to bring her some work from time to time, either shirts of sheets, so that she could make some money.

Mme. Dumont's daughters were very friendly with Jeanne because she was as modest in her language as in her behavior. She loved them so much that she would have gladly died for their sake. She often went to see the priest who always gave her good advice and reminded her of God's kindness and how he had taken pity on her, a poor child without family.

Jeanne gave everything she earned to Mère Nannette for she didn't need to buy anything for herself; Mme. Dumont provided all her clothes just as she had promised Mère Nannette the day of Catherine's death. The young girl was so careful with her clothes that Mme. Dumont sometimes asked her, "What do you do with your clothes, Jeanne, that they last so long?"

"Madame, I fold all my things in the evening and put them on the trunk. When there is too much mud on my skirts, I wash the bottom part, it saves them better than brushing, and then iron them. I check my clothes every morning and if I see the smallest tear, I mend it immediately."

"That's very good, Jeanne; it's an excellent habit.';'

"It is an easy thing to do, Madame, to take care of my clothes, because you give them to me."

(At sixteen, Jeanne was big and strong. She took care of Mère Nannette who was ailing. Nannette advised Jeanne not to live in the city, which was dangerous for young girls. After ailing for eighteen months, Mère Nannette died.)

The priest said that Jeanne behaved and spoke like an honest girl, and that Gerbaud (Mère Nannette's nephew) would certainly not allow her to remain silent, not claiming her share.

"No, reverend Father, she won't be silent with me. They all say that she cared so well for my poor aunt, as if she were her own daughter, and to show her that I'm thankful, we'll divide in half the money that we find. What do you say about it? Is this all right?"

"Yes, Gerbaud, it will be all right."

They opened the closet and first they took out eight sheets belonging to Jeanne and marked with her name. After turning everything upside down, a blue stocking was found behind a bundle of old linen, a stocking that served as a purse for Mère Nannette. It contained 150 francs.

(The priest spoke to Jeanne about finding a job.)

"If you want to find a place in town, Mme Dumont will be able to place you in a good house with high wages."

"Father, I won't move to the town, my dear deceased mother warned me against it, and though she is no longer with us, I still want to obey her."

"Since you want to stay in the country, I'll go to see the mistress of Grand-Bail. Her servant is getting married in three weeks. If she hasn't found anyone yet, I'll take you there tomorrow."

"Thank you very much, Father. They are nice people and I'll be very happy to stay with them."

When he left, Jeanne attended to the goat and the geese as she usually did. She put back into the closet all the things that were out and then she ran to the Dumonts. She told them, crying, that somebody was to talk about her with Mère Tixier, the mistress of Grand-Bail.

"She will be kind to you, my good Jeanne," said Sophie, who had been married for two years. She often heard us talk about you, and she would be very happy to have you in her house, and you'll be like a family over there. Calm down a little! Won't we still be friends?"

"Without you, what would become of me! I'll be grateful to you all my life."

Maurice's Childhood

Jérôme Ferragu, a wheelwright, was a widower with a little boy of four. He did not want to remarry, but on the other hand, he was not rich enough to take a servant; so his house was not well run. Jérôme worried when he left his son alone and went out to work all day. Women living next door used to keep an eye on the child, but they had to take care of their own families and their own children, so they could not always be busy with Jérôme's little boy. The poor man could not leave his house without regret, and while working on the farms where he was hired, he thought constantly about Maurice and worried lest an accident befall him. If the wheelwright had to sleep out, which often happened to him if he worked far from home, he could not close his eyes at night.

If not for that concern, Jérôme could have been happy. He lived in his own house, with a garden surrounded by hemp fields. His crops were sufficient to feed him, and his vineyard gave him more wine than he could drink. Jérôme was able to put aside the major part of his earnings after deducting taxes and expenses.

On St. Michael's eve, Jerome was on his way home. As he carried his tools he thought and worried about all his problems. Suddenly he heard someone crying nearby. He raised his head and saw Grand 'Biche sitting on the side of a ditch, sobbing with all her might.

(Grand 'Biche explained that she had been evicted for failing to pay her rent.)

Manon Dumaine was a young girl, big as a man, very ugly, who had never had a chance to marry, but she was indeed the best and kindest soul in the world. Her good nature, as well as her height, earned her the nickname of Grand 'Biche ("Big Doe"), and she was known only by that name. When she did not have to go out to work by the day, she always went to her neighbors to take care of their children, to clean their houses and to do their wash. The poor girl could be happy only when she was busy with others. All the little children of the village knew her very well and ran to her from afar if they saw her and called her Mère 'Biche. Because in fact, she was like a mother to all of them.

It was quite rare if, notwithstanding her poverty, she did not have some nuts, apples, or plums in her pockets to give to the children, and more than once she ate only dry bread in order to give her share to her little dears as she called them. One could always see her with a child on each arm, and two or three others pulling her by her apron. Her ugliness did not repel them, for the expression on her face was kindly.

If someone was sick and had to be taken care of, if a corpse had to be put into a shroud, if someone was needed to run to town with an urgent mission, one would always look for Grand'Biche, and never ask if it was convenient for her or not; so sure were they that she would quit anything in order to oblige, no matter whether she was paid or not.

(Jérôme asked Grand'Biche to come and live in his house, to care for Maurice and do the housekeeping. Any time she could get a day's work she could keep her wages. Grand'Biche was very happy with the arrangement.)

Everything was fine in Jérôme's house since Grand'Biche took over the management. When he came back at night, he would find his table set with a delicious soup and his child sparkling clean. Now he could sleep quietly and work with all his heart's desire. He was a different man.

12. Grand' Bîche and the children

Grand'Biche knew how to save, and something always remained from the little money that Jérôme gave her every Sunday for the weekly expenditures. She dug and watered the garden, and at snack-time, while eating her bread, she took the child on her arm and walked him to the village. Maurice pressed her head with his little hands and said, "Mother Biche, when I grow up you will be old and you won't be able to walk. Then, I will carry you in my turn."

From the very first month she asked Jérôme to get her a cow and a female goat. "We have enough to feed them and we'll have more ease in the house."

"But, Grand'Biche, if you take the animals to the fields and if you are busy making butter and cheese, you'll have no time for your paid work."

"So what? Do I have any other interests besides yours?"

When Maurice saw the goat, he said, "Mother Biche, you should make me a little sack of cloth to put my snack in and I'll go watch the goat in the fields like other children do." When the sack was ready, he tied it on his back with two strings that crossed upon his chest, and were kept in place with small pieces of wood.

Grand'Biche took Maurice to church every Sunday. She did not buy a seat, in order to save money, and used to stand or kneel. The child leaned against her as if he were looking for protection among all those people who frightened him a little, almost hiding himself in the kind girl's apron while secretly observing the newcomers.

One night Jérôme took Maurice in his lap and told him, "Maurice, you are six, it's time to learn something my little one. Do you want to go to school?"

"Papa, nothing could be better, but who will watch my goat?"

"Don't worry about that; will you study hard?"

"Is it wise to make the child study at this age?" asked Grand'Biche. "Will he stay quiet during all the lessons, this innocent child who is lively as a bird?" And saying so, she seized Maurice as if someone was taking him away from her.

"He will have to learn to be quiet. All right, my child?"

"Yes, Papa. You'll see, 'Biche, how much I'll learn!"

"Tell me," Grand'Biche went on, "why does he need to know all those things? Will it help him to work any better?"

"Yes, of course, for ignorance is a real obstacle to work."

"I don't think so. Aren't you successful in what you do; you who can neither read nor write?"

"Not as much as you think, Grand'Biche. I don't tell you how often I am cheated out of money which is due me, just because I cannot keep a record of my working days. Besides, is my ignorance any reason? My little boy has to be better off than me. Ignorant people trust no one, and they always think that others want to cheat them. Such thoughts spoil one's outlook. I don't want Maurice to suffer what I have suffered. In my day, knowing nothing was not so terrible. But now, when all the children go to school, those who know nothing will be at too great a disadvantage. Besides, one cannot be excused for staying ignorant when one has the chance to study."

"It will cost a lot, Jérôme!"

"That's possible, but this investment will bring much interest."

Maurice went to school and distinguished himself quite soon. At night, on his way home, he would walk in front of his father, carrying some of his tools for him. On days off, he worked in the garden with Grand'Biche. In the spring, M. Rémi, the teacher, gave him a dozen cabbage seedlings and the same amount of lettuce. He planted them and watered them with great care. The first time they ate soup made from one of his cabbages and picked his first lettuce for supper were days of great joy for him. The child already appreciated order and work. In the morning, before leaving, he stacked the wood, cleaned the front of the house, then dusted the furniture.

Jérôme broke his leg and would never walk again. Grand'Biche sold her gold cross to buy him a wheelchair.

After school one day, five or six large students were having fun playing marbles. They started to argue over a questionable score and became quite irate when two small boys chasing each other scattered their marbles helter-skelter over the ground. The players, already angry, became even more bad-tempered and the strongest among them grabbed and caught one child and hit him. Maurice told him, "Badouin, leave the child alone, now, or you'll have to deal with me."

"To deal with you! I'm not afraid of you; I could easily fight two of your size!"

"Leave him alone! You are good at beating up small children. You will never pick on a big one, even me. You wouldn't dare."

"Ha! Ha! You think so? Well, we'll see."

And at once Badouin let the child go and jumped on Maurice to knock him down.

"Run away, little one." cried Maurice to the child whom Badouin just released. "Run away really fast!"

He did not have to say it a second time.

"Bravo, Maurice! Bravo!" shouted all the boys together.

Badouin was ashamed of being so stupid as to release the child when Maurice was so slyly directing his attention to himself. Then, when he saw that everyone was laughing at him, he took a stone and threw it at Maurice. The stone hit him on the forehead. The whole band dispersed immediately.

Maurice came home with a large wound. Grand'Biche was sick with horror when she saw blood all over his face. "My God! What happened to you, my child?" Jérôme exclaimed. "Were you fighting?"

"No, father, I did not fight. Don't worry, it's nothing..'

"But where did you get such a blow?"

"I'll tell you." And in a few words he told what had happened. "I assure you, father, it's nothing," he said again. "I'm strong enough to endure it." "You are a brave little one," Jérôme said, hugging his son. "It's a good thing to do, to defend the weak, for you know, my boy, there's nothing meaner than to assault those who cannot stand up for themselves."

Grand'Biche let the blood flow out of the wound, then she made a compress soaked in tincture of arnica and bandaged her dear boy's forehead.

After his first communion Maurice began to feel the need to get a job. Sometimes, between classes, he went to the village blacksmith. He wanted to be helpful to the blacksmith or to the customers who brought their horses to be fitted for shoes. Maurice could chase flies or stretch wire. At other times he would throw coal into the forge, clean the shop and work the bellows if the apprentice was busy somewhere else. He often led the horses to the water trough. If he went to fetch some tobacco, or anything else, he was almost always given a coin for his trouble. Then the child would buy something for his father to eat. Jérôme scolded Maurice for spending the centimes he earned on treats, but Maurice was so pleased that tears came to his eyes.

One day, they sent Maurice to town to call the veterinarian for a sick horse and gave him fifty centimes for his trouble. The poor little one ran at once to the innkeeper, who sold groceries, and bought half a pound of sugar. His father liked plain cake dipped in wine very much, for this food sustained him best of all, but he ate cake without sugar in order to save money, and Maurice was very happy to be able to indulge him for several days. He brought the sugar to Jérôme, hoping to give him some pleasure.

Jérôme was touched so much by his son's joy and by this proof of tenderness that he did not have the heart to scold him as usual. Still, he added while thanking him, "My boy, you are not thrifty enough. You should keep the money you earn for your work, and you will buy some clothes with it, for winter is coming soon."

"Father," Maurice answered resolutely, "the best economy is to care for your health, isn't it, mother Biche? I don't need anything, and if I'm cold in winter, I'll run and jump to warm up. I want so much to see you happy, because when you are happy, we are happy too, me and my Biche! Don't you know that?"

"How do you like the little one's reasoning?" asked Grand'Biche. "You should listen to him, Jérôme, and not be upset."

One Thursday morning, Maurice was blowing Bertrand's forge while they were shoeing the horse of an ox merchant. He heard him say, "Tonight I expect a big herd to stay at the village inn. I don't have cattle-drivers to lead them tomorrow to Vierzon. Could I find them in your village? This is not my usual route, but since it is as good as the other one and shorter, I want to have my herds follow it now. Young boys in this area are not used to driving oxen and they can get scared."

"Scared!" he exclaimed, "If you want to hire me, I will lead your cattle to Vierzon."

"You, little one! You are still too young for such a rough trade. Do you know that it is four leagues from here to Vierzon? Oxen do not walk fast, it's true, but they always try to get away from the road so that one has to shout at them all the time and to run from one side to the other. Then the oxen rest at the half-way mark, and you won't be able to return here before two or three in the morning."

"What does that mean to me?" asked Maurice. Don't worry, I'll drive your cattle."

"Although the boy is young, he is not a fool," said the blacksmith, "and he is brave."

"Well then, little one, find me one of your friends who would like to come with you, but I want him to be older than you are. There will be a three-franc coin for each of you."

"I'll go and find Frisé; he is fourteen. He's not very well off either and he won't refuse the chance to make some extra money."

When Grand'Biche learned that Maurice was going to drive oxen as far as Vierzon and would not be back before dawn, she screamed and shouted that she would never allow that.

"But why not?" asked Jérôme. "He has to get used to hard labor at an early age. If I remain alive much longer I won't be leaving him much, my poor son!"

"What! Jérôme, you will let the child go at night, like that!"

"Of course, mother Biche, and I think I'll even be doing him a favor at that! Go, my child, and do not be afraid. Be an honest boy, serve faithfully for the money you earn and you'll have no problem."

"Don't worry, father. They'll say of me, as they say of you, 'He's a Ferragu, he can be trusted.' "

Grand'Biche had to give up. She put a good piece of bread and cheese into the boy's bag, and also a little bottle of weak wine. Then Maurice gave her a hug and said, "Don't be afraid, mother, nothing will happen to me I'm sure. Besides, I am not alone. Frisé is coming with me. You see," he said in her ear, "I have to earn money now so that father will no longer be in great distress. It's my turn to comfort him now. I'm not afraid of work, not at all!"

The two boys drove the oxen so well, especially Maurice, who was the more active and the more intelligent, that the merchant who followed them on horseback, was very pleased and promised to hire him again next time.

At night Jérôme could not sleep, for he worried more than he wanted to show. He heard steps outside. "Grand'Biche!" he called, "Are you asleep?"

"Oh no, of course not! I hear our little one, and I am already up. I'll light the candle."

Maurice knocked, and, as soon as he came in he ran to his father's bed and handed him the three francs that he earned. "Here is enough money to live a whole week, father!"

Ferragu gave him a hug, happy to see him so courageous and resolute. "Come on, go quickly to bed," he told him.

"As for me," said Grand'Biche, "I am going to give you a little drop of hot wine with sugar to drive away the bad night air. You did not eat?" Here is your bread and cheese just as I gave them to you."

"Of course I did mother Biche. I ate, and ate well, I tell you. When the oxen had rested in the village, which is two leagues from here, the merchant made us share his snack, and then, in the evening, he gave us a good supper in Vierzon. I ate meat, and it gave me the strength to come back."

"Come on," the good woman said while passing him his hot wine, "drink and go to bed; tomorrow morning you won't be tired any more."

The next day Maurice went to see the blacksmith as soon as he got up.

"And so, traveler, how did you like Vierzon?"

"The town seems to be rather big and pretty, with the river Cher, a channel, and another river. The merchant, when he saw how astonished I was, said that one could tell at once I had never left my village. He offered to take me to Paris when he comes by next time."

"Will you be able to go that far?"

"Well! Why not, Maurice Bertrand? And meanwhile, you must give me some work. Take me into your shop! I'll do everything you want! Say yes, little father Bertrand!"

"But you are not strong enough yet, my boy!"

"Maître Bertrand, there are not many boys of twelve who are stronger than I am, and then I'll be growing bigger daily. I liked it so much yesterday when I brought a little money to my poor father that I'd like always to make money so that he is not so unhappy."

"All right. If you want to come and blow the bellows all day, I'll give you two francs a week, but it's a tiring job, I tell you."

"That's all right with me. Thank you very much, Maître Bertrand. Tomorrow I'll be at the door of your shop before you open it."

In the morning Maurice was there waiting for the blacksmith to open his shop. Bertrand gave him a small apron made of leather with a shiny clip and he worked all day like a man. When he was not blowing, he did other small jobs and was never idle. He even took up the hammer the moment the apprentice was not there.

"You know, you are not clumsy at all," said the blacksmith.

"Sir, I want so much to learn! Let me work sometimes. You know that I am not afraid of work and I'll try my best."

"At snack time, Maurice went to see the teacher and told him, "M. Rémi, I am already twelve. I'm big and strong, and my turn has come to go to work. No one brings money into our house since my poor father has been ill for Grand'Biche can almost never leave him." Maurice explained that he had become the blacksmith's assistant.

"You are right, my child to try to comfort you family according to your means."

"But, Monsieur, the problem is that I don't yet know everything you taught me that well and it drives my father to despair, and he is easily upset."

"My friend, it is very easy to comfort him on that point. You will just have to come every night when your shop is closed. I'll have you read, write, and count."

"Oh, thank you, M. Rémi. You do me a great favor. From Bertrand, I'll learn the trade little by little, making some money at the same time, and quite soon I'll be able to comfort my father."

"Be careful, Maurice! The blacksmith is a violent man, and he won't be any kinder to you than he is to anyone else who makes him angry."

"I know, Monsieur, and I'll do everything right so he won't get angry."

When he returned to his father, Maurice told him that the teacher was kind enough to give him lessons every day for the sake of friendship. Jérôme was so happy to hear it that he spent a quiet night; something he had not done in a very long while.

M. Rémi, the teacher, liked Maurice very much. On Sundays he took him to town. Since the boy asked questions about everything he saw, and the teacher answered him in such a way as to make him truly understand everything, his mind was thus growing all the time, and his head was full of all sorts of information.

M. Rémi, surprised by Maurice's capacity to learn everything he was shown, went to see Jérôme one day and told him, "Jérôme, if you would like to push your son, he could go far. I am sure that it will be easy to have him enter a school of arts and trades."

"Monsieur, what do they learn in those schools?"

"They learn to work wood and iron with great perfection. Then they also teach all the sciences that a worker needs."

"But, Monsieur, will he be happier after such a school than if he stayed on as an apprentice at Bertrand's."

"Yes, certainly. He will be happier because his mind will be more open and because he will better understand everything he sees."

At that moment the priest came in and Jérôme asked him for his opinion.

"My opinion is that we should not push Maurice to studies of a higher level," the priest said, "because this child is his father's only consolation, and it will be cruel to send him away in the pursuit of such an uncertain result. Besides, if you continue to teach him as you do, M. Rémi, he will work with intelligence and taste, and he will earn an honest living while cultivating his mind a little."

The ox merchant was passing by and came again to see the blacksmith. He offered Maurice the chance to earn three more francs.

"Monsieur, I thank you very much, but now that I work every day I can no longer make independent decisions."

"Go drive the oxen, my boy," said Bertrand. "Three francs are worth the trouble. Tomorrow I have to go to Graçay to buy some iron, and my journeyman is working far away so we won't need the forge and I can do without you."

"Sir, thank you for your kindness."

The next day Maurice left at dawn together with Friśe. For dinner the merchant told them to sit down with him. "Do you want to go to Orléan, little one?" he asked Maurice.

"Thank you, Monsieur, I would be very happy to see such a big city and the beautiful river Loire, which is said to be larger than our whole village. However, I am like an apprentice at the blacksmith's. He needs me and I must be in his shop every morning."

"For eight days he can do without you, and your friend will tell your parents that you have gone with me."

"But Monsieur, it would be a bad thing to do to the man who employs me. If I fail to do my duty, I'll never dare show my face to my father, who has always taught me to be an honest person."

"Is he really tough, your father?"

"Oh no, Monsieur! On the contrary, but he says that the first and most important thing in the world is to have a good conscience, and if ever I do anything dishonest it will kill him."

At the end of six months, Maurice was already making three francs a week, then four francs the next year. Eventually, by the age of fifteen he was bringing six francs to his father every week.

(Jérôme weakened and died, leaving his house and possessions to Maurice and Grand'Biche. Maurice was desolate. He learned from his teacher:

"Work is the next best thing after prayer for curing pain in this life."

Maurice remained a good worker in Bertrand's shop for three years).

At the age of eighteen, Maurice said he'd like to go on the *Tour de France.** His teacher had nothing against it. "You are right, my friend, to wish to travel. An artisan who learns his trade and does it with understanding is always commendable. The desire to do one's work well will always lead to the best, so keep this desire forever, Maurice, and you will be just fine."

"Don't worry, teacher, I'll do everything to become skillful in my trade, even if I never have to use it, for the one who is able to do more can always do less."

When Maurice came to say good-by to the priest, the saintly man told him, "My poor child, you are too young to be on your own. Up until now you've been a decent fellow, but you were never exposed to any temptation. From now on it will no longer be the same. Promise me that every night you will think about everything you did during the day and ask yourself if your father would be pleased with it. That way you will always know where you are with your conscience, and do not forget, my friend, that in this world no happiness can be true if it is not pure."

Bertrand was greatly displeased with Maurice's decision for he was losing a good worker. "I wonder if you really need to roam the countryside," he said, "or if I could show you enough land here."

"Sir, I want to see the country. It gives one ideas, and also, living with many different people helps to form one's mind and character."

Grand'Biche was desperate when she learned that her dear child was going to leave her. "Don't you know enough yet that you want to roam the country and live with people whom you won't know? You could teach the trade to your master if you wanted!"

"No, mother, one thinks one is good enough if one has never left his village; then, in some other place, one finds out that one knows nothing."

"But look at those who stay. They are not unhappy, even though they have never left their homes."

* The traditional journeymen's final training before qualifying as a master was a tour of workshops in several cities where he learned to perfect his skills.

"I'm not sure, mother. Look at Bertrand! I'm sure I will like our village even more when I return."

Maurice and Grand'Biche agreed to divide the 300 francs they had. Maurice took 100 francs and left 200 for Grand'Biche to live on. She secretly put an additional 100 francs into his trunk.

CHAPTER SIX

Young Adulthood

In Section II, the differences between Jeanne and Maurice grew wider. Jeanne, wishing to be faithful to the advice of Mère Nannette, took a job as a servant in the countryside. Maurice went against the wishes of Grand'Biche and struck out on his own on a journeyman's tour of France to perfect his skills. Both Jeanne and Maurice spent several years in a new family structure: Jeanne as a daughter/servant to the neighboring Tixier farming family and Maurice as a son/journeyman to Blanchard, a master blacksmith in Paris.

Jeanne and Maurice learned new skills from their respective employers while also setting a good example to young children and other workers. In fact, both Jeanne and Maurice even gave advice to their employers. The idea that adults could learn from young adults was a new notion which Carraud aimed at the parents of the children reading these books.

Since Jeanne and Maurice were paradigms of good workers, Carraud provided two examples of how not to behave in the persons of Marguerite and Frisé. Marguerite, unhappy with her work as a shepherdess for the Tixiers, marched out on her own to earn more money and to have more freedom. She was doomed to failure. These were not values being urged on peasant girls. Frisé, on the other hand, was a lazy drunkard who was reprimanded for his lack of discipline and unwillingness to work. Both Marguerite and Frisé reformed under the guidance of Jeanne and Maurice.

Young adulthood for Jeanne and Maurice was spent learning additional skills and saving money to establish their own families. Little mention was made of sentiment; no discussion was made of role conflicts. Their characters remained essentially unchanged from childhood. Maurice's one flirtation with danger convinced him to stay forever on the straight and narrow.

Jeanne in Service

(Jeanne asked Maître Tixier to hold her 250 francs in his safe. Maîtresse Tixier was very pleased with Jeanne's work. She placed Solange, her oldest and least reasonable daughter, under Jeanne's care. One of Jeanne's fellow workers was Grand Louis.)

Grand Louis, the ploughman, was not bad at heart, but he was a difficult person. Nothing pleased him. One could try in vain to please him but he never found anything done well. The girls and the servants in the house could not stand him. He always had nasty words ready for them, and they paid him back in kind. He used to insult little Jeanne too but she never replied.

One beautiful sunny day, Grand Louis dressed up in order to go to a party at Meunet-sur-Vatan. He put on new pants and a shirt which he had never worn. His hatbox was placed on a shelf in the stable, near his bed. In order to reach it, he climbed up the cross-bar of the narrow railing set against the wall, but his foot slipped at the very moment he reached the hatbox, which slid back. As he tried to grab it he managed to get caught on the railing and tore his pants and shirt from top to bottom. He became so furious that his curses were heard in the house. The cowherd went to see what had happened and reported the scene to the girls who were standing by the door.

The village boys came to call for Grand Louis. "Wait, wait, I'm coming!" he called, quickly changing his clothes; he threw his torn things on his bed, without placing them in his trunk as was his practice.

When the boys and girls left, Jeanne, who did not go to the party because she was in mourning for Mère Nannette, went into the stable to look for the torn shirt and pants.

"Really," said the maîtresse, "you are too good if you're going to mend clothes for that surly man who spares you no more than any other girl!"

"What do you mean, maîtresse? Such is his nature, but he's no worse than anyone else. He swears sometimes at his mares and that is not nice, but does he ever beat them? Whose horses could be better groomed? He has absolutely no rival at work. Our maître knows what he's worth, and does not rely on anyone else at sowing time or any other time for that matter. If

Grand Louis were happy he would not bother us like that. But he is like me. He has no family, and that's a great misfortune."

(One day Grand Louis came in for supper earlier than usual. He complained because it wasn't ready for him. The maîtresse told him,)

"You'll always be surly, Grand Louis! You'll never change! Come here a minute! In what other house are spoons and forks cleaner than here? One would say it's silver! Did you ever see glasses as bright, linen as white, a house as clean? See! Is there a single speck of dust on the furniture or a spider-web in the corners? And who keeps everything in order, if not little Jeanne? Before she came to take Marie's place, I killed myself, and could finish nothing. Now I work less and everything manages to get completed. Only you in the whole world complain about such a girl! And who repaired your shirt and pants while you were showing off at Meunet?"

(Maître Tixier advised Jeanne to use her savings to buy the vineyard that belonged to Mère Nannette. He promised to help her take care of it. Jeanne was happy to own the land of her dear deceased).

One morning as they were getting up, Jeanne said to Solange, "Your hair is all tangled, don't you ever comb it? I never see you wash your arms or neck."

"Why should I wash what nobody can see?"

"First of all, to keep clean is important enough. Try thinking about it. Also, change your shirt every night. Do you think it is healthy to sleep in the same shirt after you were hot all day? And in the morning, do you like it to dry out on you? And your morning prayer, you don't say it very often! Why don't you ever go to see the reverend Father?"

"I'd never dare go there alone."

"Then come with me. I always go there after vespers. You'll feel peace in your heart and calm in your spirit when you return from visiting him!"

After that, every morning Jeanne and Solange said their prayers. Jeanne finally made Solange keep herself clean after repeating her advice over again. Solange became more patient when she became more content with herself. She improved thanks to Jeanne's advice, and became friendly to everyone in the house.

(Maîtresse Tixier was amazed at Solange's new character).

On wash day, Solange and Josephine, Maître Tixier's two elder daughters, were washing with the shepherdess while Jeanne soaped the sheets and put them into blueing. Then she stretched out the linen. The maîtresse, followed by her little Louise who was only eight, was walking to and fro and listened to what the girls said while working.

"My God, how happy rich people are!" the shepherdess was exlaiming. "I'd like so much to be like our maîtresse who is walking over there doing nothing while we take such pains to beat this linen!"

"So, you think she did not work in her youth," asked Solange, "and that her fortune came all by itself?"

"I'd like to have," Marguerite (that was the name of the shepherdess) continued, "many houses, vineyards, lands, and do nothing."

"All that would not last long," said Jeanne, "because having property is not all there is to it. It quickly goes to seed if you don't take care of it, and you'd never work on it—you, who do not even take care of your own clothes!"

"That's true, said Solange, "you are always torn and dirty, though you spend all your money on clothes. Look at little Jeanne who doesn't buy anything but is always neatly dressed! One would say that she always has her Sunday clothes on!"

"Maybe, but I was not brought up on charity, like she!"

Jeanne wiped away a tear.

"I won't forget that wickedness," the maîtresse said, approaching them. "Marguerite, you'll have to answer to me for that remark. Don't be upset, my Jeanne. Just because you had to beg for bread does not lower our esteem for you."

"It does not prevent us from loving you like our sister," little Louise added, and embraced her.

When the washing was dry, Jeanne showed Solange how to stretch and fold it in order to make it look ironed. When she was folding Grand Louis' shirts, she saw that they were in a very bad state. "Look here, maîtresse, how torn Grand Louis' shirts are. If you like, I'll stay up tonight to mend them, and I'll cut the most torn into pieces."

"Little Jeanne, do as you see fit, though Grand Louis does not deserve it."

"Don't say that, maîtresse. Grand Louis helps you more than your own children. I can see it very clearly and that is why I want to mend his clothes."

When Jeanne finished mending the ploughman's shirts, she chose the time when she thought he would not be in the stable to put them on his bed, but Grand Louis was sly. Knowing well that it was Jeanne who took care of his things, he watched for her. He hid himself behind the door when he saw her coming with an armful of clothes and while she was arranging them on his bed, he jumped quickly to her side. "My God!" she said, all confused.

"Ha! Ha! So it is you, Jeanne, who takes care of my things! I thank you, but since it is unfair that you work for nothing, I want to pay you."

"No, Grand Louis! You owe me nothing. My time belongs to the maîtresse and it is she who allowed me to work on your shirts."

"Did she tell you to do it?"

"I didn't say that, Grand Louis, but had she forbidden it I wouldn't have done it."

And my torn shirt and my pants! I tell you, little Jeanne, you should not act too proud, I want to give you something."

No, Grand Louis, don't give me anything. I'll never touch your things again if you pay me, because you would think I do it for the money, but to prove that it is not pride that prevents me from accepting your money, I'll tell you what I'll do. I am a poor girl and there is no one to support me in the world. If ever I have a problem, I won't ask anyone but you for advice."

"Agreed; take my hand, little Jeanne!" He stretched out a hand as huge as a bat. Jeanne put her hand on his and Grand Louis added, keeping her hand in his for a second, "I am sure you'll keep your word." Jeanne pulled her hand away and went home.

(Grand Louis worked hard to improve Jeanne's vineyard.)

The summer solstice, celebrated by the Festival of Saint-Jean, was coming close. Maître Tixier said to his servants, "It is time to decide who is going to leave and who will stay on for the coming year." Since no one spoke up, he said to Grand Louis, "Let's see, you are the eldest, are you planning to stay?"

"Maître, if you are not dissatisfied with me, I'm not dissatisfied with you, so I'll stay on if you'll keep me."

"Keep you! I think I will, my boy. There is no one to equal you in four leagues around. If you are content, I'm content also."

The cowherd and the swineherd also stayed, but Marguerite, the shepherdess, said that she wanted to hire herself out to other farmers. "Maître," she said, "will you hire me at the salary that others will pay?"

"So you don't like it here, Marguerite?" asked the maîtresse.

"I do, maitresse, but I want to hire myself out in order to have key-money. Besides, I've heard that a shepherdess can make twenty-five écus and you pay me only twenty."

"Do you believe that silly talk, Marguerite?"

"Why, Marie from the farm at Chétif-Bail told me that."

"Well then, go if you like. You won't be any great loss to us. I haven't forgotten what you said to little Jeanne."

"Let her do as she likes," the maître said, "but I warn you, Marguerite, once you leave this house you are out and I won't take you back; even if you work for no salary at all. You know me and you know that I keep my word! And you, little Jeanne, you haven't uttered a word?"

"Maître, what do you want me to say! Do I have any other home but yours? I'll leave it only when you send me away. I love you like my own father, and it seems to me that your daughters are my sisters. What else can I look for?"

"If it is like that, my girl, we won't be parting soon, but since we agreed on your wages only until Saint-Jean, you have to say what you want to earn next year."

13. Jeanne and Grand Louis

"Maître, you are a wise man. I'll take what you give me, and let's not discuss it. Look, Marguerite," Jeanne went on, "tell me why you can never stay long in one place? What pushes you on?"

"You want me to tell you? It's because my employers never like me."

"But tell me, Marguerite, did you love your employers? You don't even show a love of God. In church you talk, laugh, you show off. You don't hear a word of what the reverend Father says, and you never go to confession."

"What is the harm of that? I don't hurt anyone."

"You do harm to yourself, to say nothing of the bad example you give. Isn't church the house of the good Lord? Do you take on those airs when the maîtresse sends you to take something to Mme. Dumont's? Do you laugh or talk in her beautiful house?"

"My goodness Jeanne, I don't even dare to raise my eyes!"

"And our God who is in heaven, isn't He greater than Mme. Dumont?

Did you ever notice how those ladies behave in church where they kneel down two-thirds of the time? I'll tell you the truth. People don't like you because you cannot restrain your tongue. Believe me, Marguerite, stay with us, try to love us, such as we are, and you'll see how happy you'll be."

Jeanne's words were in vain; Marguerite wanted to leave Grand-Bail.

(Grand Louis helped Jeanne out of difficulty with a nasty neighboring farmer).

The hay making and harvest passed without any incidents. Jeanne made such good soup for the harvesters and her bread was so tasty that they swore they had never eaten so well. Starting in the morning, she drew water and poured it all over the house by the bucket full. Then she swept the floor to take away the mud and manure that everyone brought in on their boots. Whenever Grand Louis saw her at his work, he brought her water. One day he told her, "Little Jeanne, I don't like to see you tired, and for what good! You cleaned in vain in the morning and at noon there is just as much dirt."

"You are right, Grand Louis, but if I don't clean out all the garbage every day, we'll be like animals in the barn. If only there were some nice gravel in front of our door, the mud from the boots would stay there and the house would not get so dirty."

The next day he brought stones from a quarry close by and built a gravel pit in front of the door.

"You've done excellent work there," maître Tixier said during supper. "It was quite necessary and I don't know why I had never thought about it. Where did you get the idea?"

"It is not my idea, it was little Jeanne who told me that if there was gravel in front of the door, the house would be cleaner and healthier."

"My boy, you are quite right to do what little Jeanne tells you to do."

"Maître," Jeanne said, blushing, "I did not tell him to do it, he did it out of his own good will."

"That's even better, my girl."

(Maître Tixier advised Jeanne and Grand Louis to buy more land.)

All those who came to the Grand-Bail liked Jeanne because she was kind to everyone; to the poor just as to all others.

When little children begged at her door, she made them come in, cleaned them and washed their hands. If she had nothing to put on their bread, she brought weak wine so that they could soak their bread in it. In winter she baked potatoes in the ashes to warm up their poor little stomachs.

After All Saints' Day, they stayed late to crack nuts. Jeanne, who often visited Mme. Dumont, brought from her house *The Book of Practical Morals.* It was an instructive and amusing book, and she read beautiful passages from it on Sunday night.

She read very well. When the others did not understand, she gave them perfectly clear explanations, with all the patience and kindness possible.

Grand Louis had changed a great deal. Instead of offending everyone, he was kind and obliging, most of all to Jeanne. He did not go out to festivals any more and one could often see him dreaming, his elbows on his knees and his head on his hands.

It was carnival time. One morning, Grand Louis went into the kitchen where Jeanne was busy kneading bread. "Listen, little Jeanne," he told her, "I should have asked you something a long time ago, but I never had the courage. I am so sad, I have no heart for anything. I have to put an end to the way I feel! Would you like to be my wife?"

"Thank you, Grand Louis, but I don't want to get married."

"That's it! I thought so! You are too much of a young lady to marry such a rude peasant as I! And still, by God, there's no one in all the town who would love you as much."

"You should not get angry, Grand Louis. If I wanted to marry, I'd never find better than you. But the maîtresse is in bed, unable to do a thing and the poor woman has no hope of recovery. Solange will soon be asked to marry and then will go away. Josephine is only seventeen and is still too young to take full care of her mother. So, I cannot leave our much-beloved employer. Something tells me that if I do, it will be wrong."

"That's not the point, my Jeanne. We'll stay here. They will be only too glad to have us stay."

"You could be right, Grand Louis, but children would come and when one has children, it's better to live on one's own. It's difficult enough to live with one's parents, much less with strangers! But in order to prove my esteem for you, if you'd like to wait for me, I promise never to marry anyone else. I am only twenty, you are not yet twenty-six. We have time."

"As you wish, Jeanne, though I'd prefer to get married right now."

(Solange, who became an excellent young woman, married Guillaume, the son of a neighboring farmer. The wedding celebration, prepared by Jeanne, lasted for three days.)

After the wedding another shepherdess was hired so Josephine could stay at home in place of her sister. The maîtresse was very grieved by the departure of her eldest daughter, but she calmed down and soon Jeanne trained Josephine just as she had previously trained her sister, Solange. Everything went on well in the house except that the maîtresse was always in bed.

(Jeanne was twenty-three-years old. Grand Louis still wanted to marry her. He told Maître Tixier.)

"Maître, Jeanne and I would like to get married, and we're asking for your opinion."

"What are you talking about, Grand Louis? Get married! Leave me! You want to ruin me, I see! What do you want my house to become when you leave? My poor wife can't even get up. Who will take care of her?"

"Maître, don't get so excited. Listen to reason. Do you know that I asked Jeanne three years ago and she refused to marry then because she saw that the maîtresse could not do without her? The poor girl loved you too much to leave you in troubled times. But now that Josephine is able to replace her, we want to get married. We have waited long enough; for after all, youth is passing us by.

"So, it is true that you want to leave us, little Jeanne?" asked the maîtresse, who was awake and heard everything.

"My dear maîtresse, I have no parents. If I had the misfortune to lose both of you, I would never work for others, and I would never find another man like Grand Louis, whom I have loved for a long time."

Maître Tixier sat there, his head in his hands, and said nothing.

"Husband, we should let them get married on the condition that they won't leave us."

"Yes, the maître said, "promise me that you'll stay until Josephine gets married."

"Since you desire it, we'll stay with you. Right, little Jeanne?"

"But," she said, "when children come I won't be able to work as much. They'll cry. They'll bother you."

"Don't worry," said Louise, "I'll take care of them and you'll have no trouble."

"Didn't my children cry?" the maître asked, "or those that Josephine and Simon will have when they get married, won't they cry? Aren't you our child just as they are?"

"How good you all are!"

"So, it is settled; you won't leave us."

Jeanne and Grand Louis promised to stay. A month later, they were married without ceremony or fanfare. The priest who was so fond of Jeanne gave her a dinner after the nuptial mass. He invited the witnesses too, and the first among them was maître Tixier. Good wine was given to everyone at Grand Bail that night and they all drank to the health of the newlyweds.

Maurice's Tour de France

Maurice left for Bourges, passing through Issoudon. After two days he found a job with a master who gave him shelter, food, and one franc a day. Thus, he could put two francs in each of his small bags, and by the end of the month he sent Grand'Biche her share.

The master was a very skillful man. He liked Maurice and showed him all the subleties of their trade, but the great desire to learn made Maurice impatient and often was an obstacle to his work. His master asked him one day, "Have you visited our cathedral?"

"Yes, sir, and I can't help admiring it. I could never imagine a building of such dimensions."

"I want to show it to you in more detail, you will be even more impressed. I know the sacristan and on Sunday, between mass and vespers, we'll walk in the galleries and visit the roof."

When they finished their survey of the admirable construction that still looked new after six hundred years, Maurice said, "I'm not so much astonished by the fact that someone had the idea to make such a big church as by the endurance and courage that were needed in order to work that long."

"That proves, my boy, that you don't yet know the advantages of perseverance, the great virtue of the working man, which is, unfortunately, so rare, though it is one of those that bring him the most profit. You have to realize that it is not enough to have an idea . . . If the work is not completed how shall we know if the idea was good or not? How shall we ever know if one is capable of accomplishing it?"

Maurice often went for a walk with his master and some other workers older than he instead of going with his friends, who made fun of him because of that.

"We'll be old, too, in our turn," he told them, "and we won't like being forsaken. The old have worked a lot and know a lot and one can always learn from them."

(Maurice left for Paris, after six months of good work in Bourges. Following a two month journey he reached the city. Instead of going directly to the ironmonger to whom he had an introduction, Maurice wandered through Paris, amazed by the great variety of products made by craftsmen. After two weeks of wandering, Maurice was arrested for brawling in a tavern. He was released the following morning and went directly to the ironmonger who found him a job with M. Blanchard, a blacksmith.)

The poor boy was truly happy when he thought that he could put aside something for his old mother Biche whom he had neglected so long.

After a month the blacksmith received a big order for carriage wheels. All the workers in the shop refused to work for the wages they had agreed upon, in the hope that this order would force their boss to give them a raise. They tried to persuade Maurice to do as they did. "No, really, I'm not going to do as you do," he answered. "I have an agreement with the boss, and as an honest employee I'm honor-bound to keep my word."

(Maurice persuaded his fellow workers to return to work.)

That evening Maurice did not go out with the others. Instead, he entered the sitting room where all the blacksmith's family was gathered.

14. Maurice in Paris

Blanchard was there with his wife and his son, Julien, who ran the shop in his father's absence.

"Sir," Maurice said, "My friends charged me to ask you to forget about everything that happened. They are mad at themselves for their stupid behavior and they ask for nothing better than to stay in your shop."

"Ha! Ha! That's a good one! So they did not find any work in other places?"

"Sir, they did not look for work, I swear."

"He doesn't tell you," the honest boy Julien added, "that he himself brought them back to reason, calling on them for their behavior."

"So, he's not one of that gang."

"No, sir, I never failed to keep my word and I hope, with God's help to be like that always."

"Well, then, though I'm much displeased with your comrades, I'll keep them, since you ask me to do so, but tell me now, aren't you too young to live alone in Paris?"

"That's true, sir, but I have to resign myself to it."

"Listen, my boy, I noticed that you work faithfully, competently, and that you don't like to waste time. Besides, my son wants to be friends with you. Would you like to stay with us? You can sleep in a room with Julien. My wife will wash your clothes and I'll give you forty francs a month."

"Thank you so much, sir; I accept wholeheartedly, for I feel very lonely among people whom I don't know and, also, when one dines out with others, one is always driven to spend more than one intended."

"So, you know how to save money?"

"Sir, my poor father was disabled at thirty-two. I heard him so often deplore his bad luck, which did not let him save something for his old age, that I really want to put aside some money which I can use should I become ill also."

When Maurice became part of this family, which he thought was a happy one, he soon noticed an uneasiness in Mme. Blanchard's ways. He could also see that her husband's absences were not always motivated by the needs of his business, as he pretended. More than once he saw the wife secretly wiping away tears.

Maurice saw that his boss was skillful and had an abundant clientele, so he should have made a considerable profit. Several years earlier Blanchard had worked on a large order for a supply of springs and wooden rings for coach wheels. He was then considered quite a fine person, but he began to shirk his duties at the shop. Every time he went out to buy some iron or to take his records to the carriage accountant, he was side-tracked by some of his good friends who would entice him into a bar. It became a habit. He also belonged to a group of gamblers. More than once he did not return home for several days. Since he often lost more money than he had taken with him he was forced to write out short-term charges or IOUs and he was definitely not proud of it.

In the beginning his wife tried to make some suggestions which he took very badly because his friends ridiculed husbands who listened to their wives. At the time when Maurice went to live with his master's family, the clientele began to diminish in spite of all attempts by Mme. Blanchard to conceal her husband's poor behavior. However, Julien tried to replace his father in the management of the shop. He would find reasonable explanations for his absences and, above all, he did not allow the slightest mockery of him.

One Tuesday, everyone was very busy finishing a large order of springs; the master worked with fervor, for he had promised delivery by the end of that week. The iron was prepared by other workers. Blanchard, his son, and Maurice tempered it and gave it shape. They alone were expert enough to accomplish this task. The master, who had recognized Maurice's intelligence and capabilities, used him as an aid on the most difficult tasks, and soon he made a very skillful worker of Maurice.

Two of Blanchard's friends came in and one of them shouted, "What! You work here as if your livelihood depends on your own salary!"

"Is a man like you made to hit the anvil all day like a worker?" said the other. "Now, put away your hammer and your apron, quickly, and come with us to try a new kind of carriage. If it works the inventor will give you the order for springs and the firing of the wheels."

"Friends, I can't go. I have to deliver twelve pairs of springs on Saturday and they are still far from finished."

"What are you talking about? That is your workers' business! Since when does the master have to work like they do?"

"Since he is the most skillful one," Mme. Blanchard said, entering the shop.

"If our friends could see you now, Blanchard, they would scarcely recognize you as the joyful companion who usually talks and acts so well among his peers. Do come try out the new carriage on the plains of Grenell and, if there's time, we'll have a nice dinner afterwards. It's in your best interest to do so."

"Oh well then, wait for me," answered Blanchard, taking off his apron. "I'll get dressed."

"My friend," argued his wife, "the springs will never be ready for Sunday morning. The administration warned you already; you'll lose your order."

"You think so, Josephine?"

"Certainly, and besides, we won't get paid."

"Ha!" said one of his friends, "the woman always commands here! Well then, good-by. We'll know that Blanchard misses a good time because his wife does not let him go out."

"You are wrong if you think that I'm not the master in my house, and in order to prove it to you, I'm going with you. Wait for me in the bar next door. Besides, I won't be out long."

(Mme. Blanchard was very worried about bankrputcy. Maurice and Julien promised to work through the night to finish the order on time. Mme. Blanchard worked the bellows.)

On the fifth night when they were forging the last pair of springs, Blanchard, realizing that his friends were cheating at cards, left their company after losing all his money and came back home, ashamed and gloomy. It was one o'clock in the morning and he was greatly surprised to hear someone striking the iron in his shop. Since it was July and it was hot, Julien had half opened the shutter in order to let in some fresh air. Blanchard could see his wife and son working the bellows while the two young men forged and tempered the iron. He came in immediately.

"What are you doing here, all of you?" he asked rudely.

"My friend," his wife answered gently "we are finishing in order to earn the money which is to be paid on the fifteenth. For five nights these hardworking boys stayed up to finish the springs which you promised to deliver tomorrow morning. And you know they would not pay the smallest amount for an unfinished order."

"And you, Josephine, worked the bellows all these five nights?"

"Yes, she did and certainly my poor mother will be sick because of it," Julien said.

(Blanchard repented and vowed never to follow the advice of bad friends nor to enter a bar again.)

The blacksmith took the hammer from his son, who had taken his mother's place at the bellows, and he finished making the springs with Maurice. Meanwhile, his wife prepared a little midnight meal and it was almost four in the morning when they sat down at the table. Blanchard questioned Maurice a great deal about his country and his family, and when Maurice felt enough confidence in them, he said, "Sir, would you permit me to tell you something without your getting angry with me?"

"Speak, my boy. Today you have the right to say all you want."

"Well then, I'll say that I am surprised that a master such as yourself doesn't close his shop on Sunday mornings."

"What profit could I gain by doing that?"

"First, you'll be obeying God's commandment and will be able to go to pray to Him in church. Then, one day of rest out of seven is not too much for your health and, finally, people like us, constantly busy during six days of the week in order to earn food for their bodies, are badly in need of the seventh to think about their soul and to feed their spirit."

"You might well be right. I'll try it."

"I'd also like to tell you something else."

"Speak without fear. What else do you have to say?"

"There is a little apprentice who is a servant to all of your workers. Everyone sends him on errands, and he's often mistreated without any reason. Finally, and this is the worst, he is not learning the trade at all."

"What do you want me to do about it? It's always like that in shops and I don't have the time to teach that child, and Julien doesn't either."

"Will you let me teach him? He's an honest boy and smart enough. I'll make a worker of him quickly. Tell them that he's going to be my apprentice and will work only at my anvil."

"Don't worry. Starting tomorrow, he belongs to you."

Blanchard, his wife, and the two young men went on Sundays either to Saint-Cloud, or to Neuilly or else to Versailles. In a word, to all those places where there were interesting things to see. They visited all the monuments in Paris, one after another, and frequently went to the Conservatory of Arts and Trades. Sometimes, when they were too tired, they went into a bar, but Blanchard always waited for them at the door and refused to enter despite entreaties.

(Maurice worked for Blanchard for two years, then came down with pneumonia. Mme. Blanchard nursed him back to health. When he improved, he worked for a locksmith for three months, then for a grinder for three more months. Soon thereafter Maurice received a letter from his teacher telling him to return home to register for the draft.)

They had a farewell dinner, for Maurice had to take the night carriage which would bring him to Vierzon the next day. They drank to his safe trip, and when it was time to leave Mme. Blanchard put a golden ring on his finger.

"Keep it, Maurice, as a souvenir of our good friendship and for all that you have done for us."

"And since you are still so young and youth is liable to be tempted," added the blacksmith, "I recommend that you cast your eyes on this ring often. It will remind you of what an honest man can be exposed to if he does not take good care of himself."

Mme. Blanchard also gave him a small package containing an expensive flannel shirt; her gift to Grand'Biche.

(Maurice returned home to Grand'Biche.)

"My God, what a good-looking boy he is! If poor Jérôme were alive, how proud he would be to see him like this!"

Maurice cried at the memory of his father. When he calmed down a little, he said, "Mother, I came back here to see you and to bring you part of my small savings, for I owe you a hundred francs. I should have saved more, but what can I say; one likes to have some fun while still young."

"And you were right to have a good time in a proper way, my child. Keep your money, I don't need anything. I still have the hundred francs you left me and a little more besides."

"What did you live on, my poor mother?"

"I'll tell you. Since taxes on land are so high, I rented half of ours, and the garden too. I rented the hemp-field, and the income was sufficient for me. If you knew how little an old woman needs to live on!"

"Mother, I want you to be comfortable now. Look, here is a very warm shirt my master's wife sent to you from Paris."

(Maurice went to visit his teacher.)

"Tell me," said M. Rémi, "what have you learned in your travels and what knowledge have you brought home to us?"

"Monsieur, I've learned in my travels that there is no difficulty that work cannot overcome, and I have observed that the only one who is happy is the working man, for he alone can experience living at the exact measure of his intelligence. I like my trade even better now than before I left, no doubt because I now know it better and I am sure I'll find my fortune in work."

"I can see that you gained a lot from your travels, my friend. You are brave and sensible and with these qualities you will succeed."

(Maurice was drafted. The priest consoled Grand'Biche by explaining that Maurice will profit from military service.)

"He will acquire the habit of obeying strong discipline and he will learn to live with people who are indifferent to him, suffering their faults in patience," said the priest.

(Maurice sold his home and his land for 360 francs with the provision that Grand'Biche could live out her days there. The money would provide for her while Maurice was in the army.)

Maurice arrived in Austria at the time of the first taking of Vienna. He participated in different campaigns without being wounded and quickly became a quartermaster sergeant. But, having caught a fever in the swamps of the Danube, he dragged himself from one hospital to another without getting any better and finally he was sent back to France to the depot of his regiment.

When, in 1815, the army of the Loire disbanded, Maurice was in Bourges and was given his leave. He returned to his village with some savings which could have been more had he not been so generous with his friends. But, the poor Grand'Biche was no longer there to profit from his savings as she had predicted. Grass was now growing over the place where she was buried, but she died blessing her Maurice.

The teacher had removed all the furniture in the house. They found 270 francs in the old woman's closet. She had never touched the money which Maurice had left her when he went on the *Tour de France*. It had been very difficult to convince her to have a servant the last three years of her life. In her will she left all of her small possessions to Maurice.

(Maurice went to Bertrand, his old employer, looking for work.)

"Do you have any work for me, maître Bertrand?" he asked.

"No," answered the blacksmith, "I have an apprentice and don't need any more help."

"Well, then, I'll look elsewhere."

Maurice searched the neighborhood and found work in Graçay with a blacksmith who had an abundance of customers. Since he could work iron much better than most workers, his new master understood the advantage he would have by hiring Maurice and he soon proposed that Maurice marry Françoise, his only daughter, who was twenty years old.

Maurice found her to his liking, married her, and agreed that the blacksmith, who was rather wealthy, would lodge the newlyweds and would give Maurice 300 francs per year. Françoise's father wanted to make a legal agreement about property, but Maurice refused, saying that since his wife was an only child there would never be any reason for dispute and that he did not want to strip his father-in-law of the wealth he would now be earning.

Everything went well during the first year, but by the end of the second, the father-in-law caused problems when it was time to pay the 300 francs saying that the expenditures had increased because of Françoise's baby.

"Are you displeased that Charles was born?" Maurice asked.

The blacksmith did not answer but by the third year he absolutely refused to pay more than 200 francs rather than the 300 according to their agreement, because another baby was born.

This time, however, Maurice did not argue. Instead, several days later he rented a wagon to move to his old village and told his wife to pack their possessions. Françoise obeyed him, crying. She could not accept the idea of leaving her old father all alone.

CHAPTER SEVEN

Family

Carraud carefully described the establishment of a permanent home for Jeanne and Maurice, each of whom spent the first two years of married life, through the birth of second children, in an extended family. Jeanne and Grand Louis stayed with the Tixiers because Jeanne didn't want to hurt them by leaving. They left only when she feared she was becoming a burden on them because of her children. Maurice lived and worked with his father-in-law and didn't strike out on his own until the old man went back on his agreement to pay Maurice for his work. Both couples saved scrupulously and made extensive preparations for their homes.

Carraud described at length the measures taken by each couple to build a house which would be different from that of their neighbors, a house which would be less damp, cleaner, and more pleasant in which to live. She showed how they planned ahead in an orderly fashion, consulted experts, and enjoyed the results. Both Jeanne and Maurice explained to their neighbors their reasons for change and influenced them to follow suit.

Once established at home, Jeanne experienced loneliness and boredom for the first time in her life.

She slowly learned to fill her life by caring for her children (teaching her daughter to read, write, do arithmetic, and spin), and taking care of a goat and later a cow. Maurice experienced the pleasure of a man well satisfied with his work and the products of his labor. He had but to look around him, at the tangible results of a life well lived, to be reinvigorated to work more. Jeanne, on the contrary, remained happiest when others were pleased with her accomplishments. Thus, the difference between them, noted earlier, continued to grow.

Jeanne and her daughter, Nannette, developed a very special relationship. They shared the secret of Paul's (Jeanne's second son) bad character and kept his misdeeds from Grand Louis. Jeanne perceived that her daughter understood, better than her husband, her reasons for not reprimanding Paul, and she was not wrong in her judgment. Nannette was a great help to her and grew up to be just like her mother. Jeanne also developed important social relations with her women neighbors who stopped at her home to ask for advice about childcare.

In a similar fashion, Maurice taught his son Charles many skills involved in becoming a good blacksmith. He also shared with him the desire to go into the army to see more of the world and to improve himself. The latter move was opposed by Françoise, the boy's mother. Like Grand'Biche, in an earlier chapter, Françoise saw no reason for Charles to leave home.

Section 3 is witness to the growing gap between woman's world and man's world. Men don't understand things of importance to women and, likewise, women don't understand things of importance to men. Carraud socialized young girls to want to grow up just like their mothers, once their mothers had accepted new standards of cleanliness, health care, and time management; boys were encouraged to go farther than their fathers; the gap between father and sons is already visible in Jeanne's family.

Jeanne—Wife and Mother

(While Jeanne was still a servant, officers came to the farm in search of good horses. Maître Tixier offered them dinner.)

"Maître Tixier," the officer said, "you have to thank God that He gave you such rare servants. Do you realize how good your food is? I have never eaten anything better than this stew or this rich fricassee.

"That's because Jeanne is such a fine cook."

When roast turkey was served, the officer exclaimed, "What! We're not finished yet?"

"And then pie, and the crayfish, and the plain cake, and finally the dessert. Jeanne sees to it that nothing is lacking."

"It's really too much! What will you do then, maître Tixier, when you marry off your daughters if you make a meal like this for two guests?"

"I wouldn't do anything different, Sir, only instead of one pie we would have forty, instead of one turkey, I'd put fifteen on the table and the same with everything else. Then we would knock in the bilge of two casks of wine in order to drink it sooner."

"Heh! Heh! So, such are the ways here! And when will you marry off the pretty blond who is serving me this plate?"

"If maître Tixier will listen to me," said Étienne Durand, a sergeant-major, "and if Josephine has not forgotten her old friend, Tiennaud, who liked to see her jump when she was small, it will be arranged very soon. If you would please wait for me, Josephine, you will not regret it. You will be happy with me."

"Don't take this as a refusal, Etienne," maître Tixier said. "You are a fine man and I like you, but I am forewarning you that I need a son-in-law who will live with me."

"Exactly! Our family place is overcrowded, so we couldn't stay there. Look at me, Josephine. Are you frightened of me? Why are you turning away?"

Josephine blushed and did not answer, but Jeanne said, "Etienne, come back when you finish your army service and don't worry about the rest."

Jeanne had a little girl. She did not try to conceal her joy, though Grand Louis wanted a boy. He grimaced slightly, but when he had kissed little Nannette (for Jeanne wanted to name her daughter after the excellent woman who had been a second mother to her), he was so delighted that he did not think about a boy any more. The child was baptized and Louise was her godmother, together with Guillaume, her brother-in-law.

Little Nannette was so sweet, so quiet, that no one ever heard her cry. When she was contented, they would put her on the bed beside the maîtresse and never held her in their arms.

"Well, well," maître Tixier used to say, "this child was supposed to split my head with her crying and I have not heard her yet. You put her on the bed like a stump. If she were wicked you would all be around, but since she is so gentle you don't pay any attention to her at all. It's always that way!"

"You are right, father," Louise said, "but Jeanne does not allow me to pick her up."

"Don't listen to her, my girl. I'm telling you to take the child for a walk."

"But maître, she will get used to it and she will no longer want to remain in bed."

"Isn't that a shame! You are four women here and you aren't able to hold the baby one after the other? If it were Josephine's child you would not leave her alone that way!"

"But maître, it is not at all the same!"

"And I tell you that it is! Do you hear me!"

Etienne Durand returned after eight months as he had promised. He passed through Grand-Bail before returning to his father's, so anxious was he to see, with his own eyes, if Josephine was waiting for him. They were all happy to see him again, and a month after his return the marriage was celebrated on his parents' farm, which was only a quarter of a league from Grand-Bail.

One day Jeanne said to her husband, "Grand Louis, Josephine is married, we have a baby, we will probably have another. We must think about moving out, husband. We are starting to become a burden in the house."

"I think you are right, my wife, but where shall we move?"

"I would like to build a little house, very clean, very suitable, with a garden in front of it. What do you say?"

"I say that it will cost us a lot, but we would be better off and also, people who live on their own show a better image to the world."

"Listen, Grand Louis, we should build it on the lot of land that I bought from father Colis. It's very close to the road and the land is excellent. It won't take us long to have a fine garden and a hemp field. Let's discuss it with our maître!"

Tixier said they were correct in wishing to live by themselves but that there was plenty of time to think about it.

"Not so much really, maître. We should begin working on it now. You can't plant a house as you do a tree."

The next Sunday they all went together to see the field. Jeanne explained how she wanted the big room to be raised over the sty, which had to be dug two steps down in order to make it warmer in the winter, and that she would ask Mme. Isaure, who got married at almost the same time, to draw up a plan for the house.

"Let's all three of us go there," maître Tixier said.

When they arrived Mme. Dumont showed them different plans of houses. Jeanne chose one of them that had a little porch ten feet on the side and a balcony in the front, and the roof overhanging one meter all around the house to protect the porch and the balcony. The house had a sty in the basement and a cellar, also dug two feet, and then it had a little corner in the sty which did not usually exist in peasants' homes and which Jeanne valued a great deal for the sake of cleanliness. Above were two rooms and a little staircase to go to the garret; for Jeanne found it ugly for a woman to climb a ladder. But they needed at least fifteen hundred francs to build such a house and Grand Louis considered it too much of a burden on his purse. Maître Tixier told him, "Don't be concerned, Grand Louis. I'll lend you seven hundred francs for seven years and, since I intend to be repaid, I'll have you earn this money. That way, you'll be able to have some money to get started."

"My God, how good you are, maître!" Jeanne exclaimed. "When I move into our house, I will always remember that my happiness is a result of your generosity."

When they returned home, Maître Tixier said, "Since you want to build a house, my children, start immediately. In order to have a healthy house you'll have to let it dry out at least for a year. Grand Louis, it is not time for hay making yet. Take advantage of the time while there is not much to do here and get your materials now."

"Maître, I want to hire father Darnaud. He has a good horse and he will bring all that is necessary. It is not fair to use the time you pay me, for myself."

"But, I tell you it is fair to help a good servant who has been working for me for fifteen years. I don't want you taking any horses but mine."

Maître Tixier had the hay mowed in Jeanne's field, and workers could begin laying the foundation. The construction was going on and when Jeanne had nothing to do she walked little Nannette to the construction site. If the workers did not understand Mme. Isaure's plan, she explained it to them.

After the harvest the building was put up, but they did not plaster the stone walls in order to let them dry out thoroughly until the next spring. When the roof was up, Jeanne decided it was time to dig the garden so that it would be ready for autumn planting. "I want to have many fruit trees," she said, "of different kinds. Those on both sides of the alleys will cut the garden into four squares. I want peach trees along the southern wall and a vine-trellis to climb up the balcony."

"What will you do with all those trees, my Jeanne?" the maître asked.

"One day they will bear fruit. Nannette will sell the fruit in town and it will be her project. You will see how proud she will be to bring you her first peaches!"

"And how will you prevent your cattle from turning your garden into a wasteland?"

"Oh, but the door of my sty opens to the west. We'll close the backyard and no animal, not even a hen, will come into the garden. Your son-in-law gave me this idea when I told him that I don't want to have manure in front of my door to infect my house. Do you really think, maître, that the townspeople would suffer in the least if they planted grapevines and trees along their walls like they do in Normandy where Durand stayed? The village is so dirty we don't always know where to walk. It is not healthy for children, all that rotten straw and its stink! How can they learn to be clean among all this garbage?"

The Dumont family came to see Jeanne's house when it was finished. They spoke about planting, and M. Dumont said he had so many young plants in his nursery that he would provide all the trees that were needed.

"And I'll bring strawberries to you," said Mme. Isaure. "You can plant them along your lanes."

"If you want my advice, little Jeanne," M. Dumont said, "you should tell your husband to paint all the timber exposed to the air. It will cost you quite a lot because you have so much, but in principle, you'll save. The paint protects timber from worms and from rotting. Besides, Grand Louis can buy ochre by the pound and used oil, then he can mix the color himself and paint. It is not very difficult to do."

"Yes, Monsieur. He's not lazy; he'll do it."

By Saint-Jean of the next year they plastered the walls and the ceilings to make the rooms warmer. During the winter Jeanne gave birth to a boy whom his godfather, maître Tixier, named Sylvain, and she felt it was now time to leave Grand-Bail. Though Etienne Durand, who supervised nearly everything on the farm, was always good to her and her husband he would eventually grow tired of their children. Jeanne often stood in the doorway gazing at her house. Louise told her, "My, how you want to be there already!"

"It's true, my Louise, I love you with all my heart, but, the desire is stronger than I am. When I realize we are going to be in our own house it seems as if my heart will burst from joy. It's so wonderful to have one's own home and to say to yourself that you have a shelter till the end of your days!"

"What about the furniture, little Jeanne? Do you know that your old bed and mother Nannette's wardrobe won't look good in those white rooms?"

"That's what worries me; I don't dare to speak about it to Grand Louis. Men don't understand how important clean furniture is to a housewife. He spent so much money on the construction that it wouldn't be wise to mention anything more. Nevertheless, because your father advanced him some money we could still afford a wardrobe and a bed."

"Well then, I'll talk to him at supper, don't worry."

In the evening Louise said to Grand Louis, "Are you planning to keep Jeanne's ugly bed and her old trunk in your beautiful new room? It would really look awful. Everyone will laugh at you. They'll say that on the outside you are playing the pompous one with your house, which is so different from the others, and that inside you don't have anything on which to even lie down to sleep."

"You are quite right, my Louise. I've been thinking about it for some time. I know that Jeanne wants to have new furniture, though she doesn't say a word and I am happy only when she is happy. We'll need a bed, a wardrobe and polished chairs. Her old trunk can serve as a kneading-trough."

"And where do you want her to put the linen that will be changed every week after she rinses it in water? There'll be no place for it in the garret and I hope you don't want to drag it into the house."

"But do you think it would be right, Louise, to buy furniture when I already owe so much money to your father?"

"Come now," said maître Tixier, "are you bringing that up again?

Didn't I tell you, stubborn head, that I'll have you earn it? You'll have it right there in the palm of your hand; I won't take it. This is the reward I want to give to you! Are you too proud to accept it graciously? Besides, you know well that I never refuse a friend in a difficult situation. I only want to be reimbursed on the fixed day, for I value punctuality more than anything."

The next Thursday maître Tixier took Jeanne to town to buy her furniture.

"Father, Louise said, "let me come with you. I'd like to choose the bedclothes with her."

"And little Nannette?"

"I'll wrap her up and carry her like Jeanne carries Sylvain."

On the way, father Tixier told Jeanne, "At least don't you be foolish! I want you to order everything you need. Besides, I'll be there myself and we'll look carefully!"

When they came to the carpenter Jeanne ordered a beautiful walnut wardrobe, a bed, a table and a kneading-trough of the same wood, and the carpenter said he would also give her a pinewood table in the bargain.

"And a mill to sift your flour?"

"Maître, it's not necessary at the moment. You will let me sift in your house. It will be some extra work for Grand Louis because he will have to carry the sack, but that's all."

"I won't hear of it. You order a pretty mill to match all the other furniture. I don't want anything to be lacking in your house."

They chose six walnut chairs and maître Tixier also bought a matching little armchair and said it was for his godson when he grows a little larger. Then they went to the fabric merchant to get some bedclothes.

"I wish we could buy green serge," Jeanne said to Louise, "it's more padded, but I don't have enough money."

Finally they chose a beautiful red striped cotton cloth. Louise forced Jeanne to take a pretty calico painted with blue flowers on a white background to make the lining for curtains and a quilt, and last, they chose a good woolen blanket. They also bought all kinds of minor things which are necessary in a household.

"Look, my Louise! I had two hundred francs with me and now I have only ten left. How expensive it is to start your own house!"

"What do you expect. my poor Jeanne? You start only once in your whole life. But you are so clean, so careful, that all your furniture will always look like new."

Jeanne paid a skillful seamstress to make her curtains and her bedclothes. She wanted them to be ready as quickly as possible.

"Jeanne, why are you in such a hurry to move into your house?"

"Because it is time. With two children now I don't do anything in your house. I hardly earn my bread. I must put an end to it and move into my own place between the harvest and the grape gathering while Grand Louis won't be busy."

When the furniture arrived and was put in its place Grand Louis said to his maître, "Your house is full while that one over there is tired of being empty."

"Which means that you can't wait to move there. It's natural, my children. Arrange it between yourselves, but, I am warning you that I'll need you until the grape gathering is over."

"Won't I always be ready to serve you over there just the same as being here?"

"Little Jeanne, I'm letting you know too that I want to give a housewarming the same day when you have your house consecrated and I will pay for the supper. You have heard me!"

Jeanne moved her linen and clothes little by little and put them in their new places. Louise helped her whenever she could, and soon only the bed had to be transported, for Grand Louis had already moved the trunk and Mère Nannette's wardrobe. It was agreed upon that Sunday morning they would move the bed and at night the priest would consecrate the house.

The Dumont family came to see Jeanne on Tuesday, for she had told them the day before that she had moved.

"You know that you are very nicely settled, little Jeanne," Mme. Isaure said, "and what do you have in your backyard?"

"Nothing as yet, madame. Maître Tixier is going to give me a female goat, a rooster and two hens."

"He should rather give you ducks and a drake," Mme. Dumont said. "I'll send you a rooster and two hens of my best breeding."

"And I will bring you a couple of those pretty pigeons you love so much," said Auguste, who had become a handsome officer.

"And I will give you a pretty cat with long fur to keep you company," said Mme. Sophie, "because you'll find your house too big, my poor Jeanne, when you are by yourself all day long."

"Oh! I'm going to look for work as soon as I wean Sylvain. When you need someone, please, don't forget about me."

"And little Nannette, what will you do with her when you go to work?"

"I'll take her and her brother to Grand-Bail. They can stay around the house. Nannette will watch her brother while Louise will keep an eye on both of them."

"How fresh he is, your Sylvain! Jeanne, if I have a baby, you'll nurse it for me," Mme. Isaure said.

"With great pleasure, my dear lady. Command here as in your own house."

Mme. Sophie was right. Jeanne was not used to so much tranquility. It seemed to her that she was doing nothing. After she had cleaned the house, walked the goat and brought her some grass, the rest of the day seemed endless to her.

She used to spin on the balcony while Nannette was playing with her brother. When she got bored she took the two children and went with them to Grand-Bail. There, she helped Louise and quite often they asked her to stay for supper, together with her husband who was threshing in the barn. On other days she was busy with her garden. Nannette followed her everywhere, and since the mother taught her many things the little girl could talk much better than other children in the village.

When Jeanne's old neighbors passed her house on their way to the market they often went in, visited the house, then said, "This house probably cost you a lot, little Jeanne!"

"Why do you think so?"

15. Jeanne with Nannette and Sylvain

"Because you have a beautiful garden in front of it. There's neither manure nor dirt in front of your door. How do you intend to manure your fields?"

"I have enough to manure my fields without keeping the dung under my windows and infecting my house or making my children sick! Don't I have a backyard with a sty?"

"But if you don't have rotten straw in front of your door, the few cattle you have won't be enough to manure your fields."

"So, you think that the straw you spread in front of your door makes a good fertilizer? You are greatly mistaken. It only spreads sickness and fever to you and your children and nothing more!"

"How do you go about it then?"

"I put a layer of straw and one of marl over my dung every time Grand Louis cleans the sty. This way I prevent it from drying out and both the marl and the straw become an excellent fertilizer. Throw litter for your cattle up to their bellies and keep the area clean in front of your door and you'll see how well it will make you feel!"

"Who taught you all this, Jeanne?"

"Etienne Durand, maître Tixier's son-in-law from the Grand-Bail."

"So, he wants to change all the customs?"

"He doesn't want to change; he only wants to do better and he knows how. Grand Louis says that he is an excellent farmer."

Jeanne wanted very much to have a milk cow. She often talked about it to her husband, who used to say, "My poor wife, you are taking care of two children, soon you'll have three. If Mme. Isaure gives you her baby it will make four, so I'm asking you if you'll be able to take care of a milk cow!"

I'll take that poor mère Henri to help me. She begs her bread and she will work for little pay. She will watch my cattle in the fields, then she will pick up grass. I'll have only to milk the cow and the goat, take care of the milk, and you will clean the sty at night. Because, you see, I want my milk cow to be clean. I'll have her curried every day like Etienne Durand does in the Grand-Bail. I noticed that when their hides are shiny they give more, and better quality, milk."

"If you are going to get some help, that's different, because I don't want you to kill yourself with work, and I mean it!" Grand Louis told his wife they would buy her a milk cow and that maître Tixier would choose the cow himself. Jeanne was very happy. She led her cattle out to graze as often as she had done in the past at Mère Nannette's. Her daughter led the goat and little Sylvain followed them.

The year passed well and the crops were good. Grand Louis piled his sheaves tightly in a corner of the barn at Grand-Bail. He made his wine together with maître Tixier, for whom he was still working. He paid back the first hundred francs on time and earned enough to pay off a good share of the debt to Colis.

Jeanne gave birth to another boy whom they named Paul. She nursed him without too much fatigue. Paul was eight months old when Mme. Isaure came to Jeanne and told her, "I am going to give you a nursling soon, my good Jeanne. Your Paul will be only nine months old when you receive my baby. I don't want you to nurse both of them at the same time; though you are strong you would soon be exhausted. If you want to put your boy out to nurse I'll pay for him."

"Thank you, madame, but I'll wean him. He is very strong and eats already like a little man. I promise you he won't take your child's milk."

"I believe you, Jeanne. You are an honest woman; you wouldn't deceive anyone, especially me. So prepare yourself to receive your new baby soon. We shall spend the winter here, but tell me, why don't you hire a young girl to help you? You cannot do it all."

"Madame, mère Henri already works for me half a day. I'll keep her. The poor woman is so unfortunate, but courageous. I'll be more secure with her than with a girl of twelve or thirteen."

"Then I'll pay mère Henri over and above your pay."

"Pay me, my dear lady! Are you going to pay me? Oh, don't do such a disgraceful thing to me!"

"But, little Jeanne, isn't it fair if I pay you for the trouble you have with my baby?"

"My reward, Madame, will be to do you a favor and to pay back, as well as I am able, the many obligations I owe you. What would I be without you? Don't pay me, please! Let me show you how much I am attached to you and that I haven't forgotten what you have done for me. If you pay me I will think that you don't respect me at all," Jeanne added, crying.

"Don't cry, my good Jeanne. You are right. I should not pay you. Besides, money is not enough to compensate a good nurse's care, but still, I want to pay mère Henri because if I give you nothing I cannot allow you to spend money for me."

Two weeks later Mme. Isaure entrusted Jeanne with her daughter.

Women of the village often came to ask Jeanne for advice because she knew more than they did and was always ready to oblige. Watching her dress her children, they would say, "What! Jeanne, you comb your little ones and wash them as if they were bourgeois children."

"Just because they are peasants is that any reason to leave them dirty? See how clean their heads are! No sores! It's no great bother for me to wash their little bodies when they get up in the morning or to brush their hair. It is quickly done and thus I save them many little troubles. If you did the same your children would feel better and would not cry so much."

"Well, we shall try. Then tell us too, how do you keep their clothes so clean, as if they were new?"

"I fold them when the children are in bed, put them in piles on the chest, and I put their bonnets away for the night to prevent them from flies."

"Don't your little ones get soiled?"

"Of course! But I watch them. First, I don't let them eat all the time, and when eating, I put a cloth in front so that their clothes do not get dirty. I don't have to wash them so often and it saves me time and soap."

Mme. Isaure came every day to see her little daughter, who grew very fast, and she thanked Jeanne for the care.

"My dear lady, if you could know how happy I am that you don't think I took your child into my care for my own interests! I love her like my own. I don't make any distinction among them."

(Jeanne returned Mme. Isaure's little girl. She was delighted by the cow the Dumonts gave her. Nannette had trouble with her eyes and the doctor recommended that she stay out of the sun for several weeks).

Nannette was somewhat bored with doing nothing. Her mother gave her some thick hemp to spin. She began to teach her the Catechism, which did not take long for the child had a very good memory. She tended little Paul when her mother went out to work and Sylvain was at school. The little girl needed all her patience to put up with Paul's whims. He had a very bad character and never tried to please. It was a great distress for Jeanne, but she hoped he would improve when he grew up. She never lost her temper with him and was always sweet to him, but the child was insensitive to that. He never showed her any affection and came to her only when he wanted something, quite sure he would get it. He was afraid only of his father who got angry when he saw him torment Jeanne all the time. And if Jeanne cried, seeing Paul so different from his excellent older children, Grand Louis felt like beating him in order to correct him, but his wife always stopped him. Even so, small though he was, Paul sometimes had such insolent answers that Grand Louis, who was not very tolerant, gave him several good slaps. Jeanne, fearing that his little heart would harden still more, thought that only great tenderness could warm it. She began to hide all his faults from Grand Louis.

Nannette understood very well her mother's distress. Sometimes she tried to console her. "My poor daughter, there is no comfort for a sorrow like this. If your brother is worth nothing when he grows up it will be the misfortune of my whole life. My child, we have to carefully hide his bad temper and toughness. You see, there is no greater wealth than a good reputation and it begins when life begins. If people knew how bad Paul is, any future improvement would be in vain. People would say he isn't worth much, so don't tell anyone about it, not even our best friends or the priest."

"Yes, mother, don't worry! Besides, since God gave him to us, such as he is, we have to love him as he is because he is very unhappy in his heart."

With her gentleness and patience Nannette finally taught a prayer to Paul. She also made him count twice a day and, whether he wanted to or not, he learned all that a child of his age could learn, for he was smart enough and, since he was bad only at home, other people liked him. He was attached to his sister more than one would think he could be.

Nannette's eyes finally recovered because she had been docile and always did what the doctor and the priest told her to do.

(Everything went well with Jeanne and her family. Nannette made her first communion. Sylvain was an excellent student. Then, a storm destroyed all the crops. Jeanne and Louis spent a long and hungry winter without telling anyone of their troubles. Maître Tixier and the Dumonts were angry when they discovered the distress of Jeanne and Louis, but the latter believed in self-reliance. They knew there were others more in need of help).

Then followed three years of fertility. Grand Louis got back his two IOUs from père Colis, who died shortly after. Jeanne, having no other debts to pay, lived in plenty and could even put something aside. Nannette was fourteen. She could read perfectly, write, and count, and ran the house as well as her mother, who thus had the opportunity to go to work every day. Sylvain stayed with the priest. Paul went to school and studied well, but his character did not improve. He brought despair to the family and seemed to have no remorse over it.

One day when Jeanne was tossing hay for maître Tixier, she heard a loud noise from the farm. Everyone was running and shouting. Fearing trouble, she ran with the other women. When she arrived at the house she saw people standing together and went to look, too. They were all so busy that no one paid any attention to her. Suddenly, she gave a shriek, for she saw her husband lying on the ground, unconscious, his head split open. She fell upon him, incapable of uttering a word. Someone went to call the priest, who saw at once that there was no hope. He said, though, that the doctor should be called at once. They tried to explain what happened. Grand Louis had climbed up on the stand in the barn to move aside what was left of old provender and make room for the new hay when a board toppled over and he fell down on the wheel of a cart, which someone had left there, and split open his head.

They put the wounded man on a stretcher, on a feather bedding, and carried him to his house. His wife followed, choking with tears. The priest washed the wound and bandaged it while waiting for the doctor. They made Grand Louis sniff vinegar. He opened his eyes and met the eyes of Jeanne who was looking at him and crying. "My poor wife," he said to her, "it's the end, I can feel it. My body is broken. Don't cry too much. In your sorrow the good God above has taken pity on you and makes me die with a blow instead of keeping me in bed for a long time. You would have spent everything on my care and would be left in misery and poverty."

Jeanne embraced him, but could not answer.

(Louis died and Jeanne was overcome with grief.)

The priest told her, "Jeanne, your sorrow is too great to be Christian. It's a revolt against God's will."

"Father, you don't know all my misfortune! I'm going to have another baby, a poor little one who will never see his father!" and she began to cry again.

"That is another reason to calm down, Jeanne. In your desolation you are thinking more of yourself than you should. At this moment your husband is receiving a reward for his honest life and he doesn't need to be pitied. All the misfortune is with you and with your children. They will suffer if you think only about your grief. God does not want us to forget the living for the sake of the dead. That is a great sin and I don't think you want to offend God."

(Grand Louis was buried by the whole village. Tixier promised to help Jeanne. She replied)

"I am sure you will always be kind, maître Tixier, but who can give me back my dear man whom I loved so much! We never argued, we always lived in peace. Our household was a true paradise!"

"My girl, since it is God's will that you be separated, you must accept it."

Maurice — Family Workshop

The next day Maurice loaded the wagon with packages belonging to Françoise. These packages contained a great deal of linen because her father had given them a share of his since his own house was already well stocked. He told his wife to climb up on the carriage and he passed the two children to her. Then, upon getting up in his turn, he took one child from the crying Françoise. She was crying because she did not have a chance to kiss her father. He had left for work at dawn and had not yet returned.

"Don't be so upset, "Maurice told her, "we aren't going far from Graçay. Besides, we could stay here twenty years and not be able to save anything. We have to think of the children. I still have my father's old furniture, and that of Grand'Biche, and I also have their linen, so we won't have to spend any money for the moment. Later, we'll plan to furnish our place more comfortably. I'm going to rent a room for us and a shack in which to put my forge. Soon I'll have more work than I can possibly do."

When he entered the village, everyone gathered around and were happy that he came back to settle here. In the yard of an inn he found an isolated room and quite close to it was an old stable where he placed his forge. After he moved his family in, he went to Vierzon to buy all the things he needed for his trade.

After paying the bricklayers and paying for the iron, coal, and tools, as well as buying a supply of flour for several months, he had only ten francs left for his wife. Françoise, who had never known financial difficulties, began to cry. "Don't worry, my good Françoise," Maurice told her. 'We won't lack for the necessities, I promise you. You can rely on me. As though I would ever like to see you and the children unhappy!"

All of Maurice's old friends gave him their orders and brought him several farmers from the neighborhood. At the mansion they ordered railing from him for the steps and were very pleased with his work. His intelligence and skill were so appreciated that he received all the orders for locks and coach building. His work for the mansion made him known in the entire area and soon he had to take on a worker. Françoise, for her part, was frugal and hard working.

All went well in the new household, but still Françoise, who was always sad because of the quarrel with her father, had no peace of mind. Her husband kept telling her, "Just be patient, my wife. Orders keep coming rapidly to my shop and the money to your coffer. Rest assured, one day you'll have a pretty house. Isn't anything possible for those who are willing to work?"

"If I only had a cow!"

"If you need only that to be happy, you'll have one at the next fair, and a goat too. I'll rent a shed for them and you can do whatever you like with your milk. It will be your concern."

On the first day of the new year, Maurice said to his wife, "Françoise, I have no peace of mind since I quarreled with your father."

"Me neither, Maurice. I always feel a deep grief which I cannot overcome."

"Your father is angry with us. He doesn't want to make peace even though it was his fault. We have to yield, my wife. We should not start the year on cold terms with each other. I'm going to borrow a cariage and go to Graçay. Get the children dressed, they are going to learn to love their grandfather."

(Maurice and his father-in-law made peace. Six years of prosperity passed and Maurice was ready to buy land and build a house).

To build a house Maurice chose a slope which went down to a creek and overlooked the road, just at the entrance to the village. The day after he bought it he laid the foundation. He traced the yard so that it opened to the West onto the road, and he placed the house on the rising ground facing south. The wheelwright saw him at work and said, "Are you going to put up your house in the full sun like that? You won't be able to stand it on Saint-Jean's Day."

"Saint-Jean's is quickly over, Cordier, and I'm not afraid of heat. What I'm looking for first of all is to make my house healthy and I've seen that in all regions, that are not warmer than ours, the houses exposed to the south are the most salubrious and the brightest."

"You think that is why my children were sick?"

"It could be nothing else, my poor Cordier, other than the humidity in your house. (They all had scrofula.) If I were in your place I would open a window to the south and at least the sun would dry out the terrible humidity. That is the only way to save little Jacques, your last child. Otherwise, I fear that his fate will be the same as the others."

"Maurice, you frighten me! I'll do as you tell me. My God! If my poor wife who is no longer young were to lose her little boy, she would die!"

So Maurice's house faced south, raised on four steps, the gable overlooking the garden, which was on the eastern side behind the yard. He extended his building in the direction of the road and, first, built up his forge which stood adjacent to the house, then a large barn with a gateway to keep the ploughs, carriages, and other objects on which he worked.

As soon as the house was finished Françoise wanted to move into it, so impatient was she to be, at last, on her own. But Maurice, being prudent, could not agree to that. "My wife," he said, "nothing can be more dangerous than living in a house that has just been built. Its walls emit a strong coldness which causes rheumatism and other sorts of illness, and the children would be the first to fall ill. Do you want to run the risk of having them sick?"

"What are you talking about, Maurice? All that is just your own idea. Many people move into their houses even before they are finished!"

"And how many of them complain of rheumatism, at all ages! How many scrofulous children! Françoise, health is precious to everyone, but even more so to people who work for their living. Illness not only makes them suffer like everyone else, but it ruins them and, in my view, those who neglect the means to preserve their health are guilty toward their families. When one has only one's own hands to rely upon, one has to take great care to keep sickness away from the house. If it enters a house, one is lost. Our house will dry during the winter and spring. We'll plaster it for Saint-Jean and we'll move in at the end of autumn."

The neighbors repeated, in vain, that it was very silly to pay rent when one had an empty house waiting, but Maurice stood strong. He had his garden planted and cultivated so that he would find it all in bloom when it was time to move into the house.

(Bertrand, Maurice's old employer and now his neighbor, was angry and jealous of Maurice's success.)

Before Maurice returned to live in the village the old blacksmith was the leader in the whole region. It was at his door that people used to gather during snack time and on summer nights when they finished their work. He gave his opinion on everything and people asked for his advice in times of trouble. Now Maurice gained this position because of his knowledge and also because one never saw him in the tavern. Women gathered in Françoise's kitchen. Sometimes they even worked there during the day. Bertrand's house was now forsaken.

In order to forget his loneliness he went to see his neighbor, the tavern keeper, more often. He always found someone there to talk to. His sons acted the same way, and because he was not in his shop as often, people went there less frequently.

(With enormous patience, following the advice of the priest, Maurice eventually won over Bertrand and they made peace. Maurice kept his accounts in perfect order. He accepted services from many of his clients instead of monetary payment. This worked to the advantage of both. One day, Maurice's best worker was injured by a horse. Maurice and Françoise cared for him assiduously.)

"My boy," Maurice said when Felix tried to thank him, "you'll give it back some day to one of your workers. For you see, a good assistant has to be treated like a child in his master's house."

One day Charles lost his patience when forging the iron parts for a plough which he found hard to mold, and after beating on the iron for a long time, unable to give it the shape he desired, he threw down his hammer and shouted, "I'll never finish this!"

"Bah," Maurice said calmly, "doesn't one accomplish everything one wishes?"

"Oh no, Father, one does not always do what one wishes."

"No, not if one does not try hard enough, but through sustained and well planned work, one can accomplish anything and nothing else is more satisfying than a conquered difficulty."

"Oh, Father! I hate to contradict you but you are mistaken. One cannot accomplish everything one sets out to do."

"What is this all about?" the teacher asked as he entered. "I think Charles is rebelling against his temper and what he lacks is perseverance. I was somewhat that way myself in my youth, and then I recognized my fault, so I say that with willpower one can do anything."

"But after all, Father," Charles said, "I'm still not strong and I can't do much by myself."

"If you feel that you are weak, my child, don't work above your strength. I don't mean to put you through an ordeal. Work patiently, it will take you longer to get the work done, but, eventually, you will finish it."

"Charles," the teacher said, "there is something much weaker than you, and yet with time has accomplished a great job."

"What is that, Monsieur?"

"Have you noticed the big stone under the church spout on the side of the school?"

"Yes, Monsieur. It is where we would go to play marbles after class because the hole in the middle of the stone was very convenient for the bull's eye for scoring."

"And that bull's eye, as you call it, do you know who made it?"

"No, Monsieur, I never thought about it."

16. Maurice and Charles working together

"I'm going to tell you now. It's from a small drop of water which falls continuously on that slab. It is weaker by far than you and the cobble stone is as hard as iron but, through hitting the same spot, it eventually wore the hole in the rock with which you are so familiar. So, you can see what constant work can do!"

Charles was struck by the effect produced by a drop of water on a rock. He went back to his task with renewed patience, took his time, and accomplished the fitting easily. When he had finished he proudly showed the work to his father.

"You see, my child how pleased you are when you accomplish something. It is one of life's greatest pleasures. There are always people who will work to improve this satisfaction and the more intelligence and effort the work requires, the more satisfied and happy one is when it is finished, and done well."

(Maurice was injured, and during his convalescence he had time to think about life.)

"When I look at my shop with all its supplies, when I look at my well-furnished house, when on Sundays I see my children well dressed and I take them to mass with their mother, when I think that this rugged hand produced all this well-being, my heart fills with joy and my heart feels ready to burst."

"Isn't there a bit of pride along with this job?" the priest objected with a smile.

"My word, Father, I don't want to think that. I can tell you that I know I'm not better than anyone else. I'm not the only worker who puts his heart into his work and there are others who do better work than I do, particularly in the larger towns, but I cannot help being satisfied when I see that I have brought happiness to those I care for."

"So, nothing is lacking in your happiness?" asked M. Lenoir. "I'm ashamed to confess that during the first few days when I was in bed unable to do anything, I was involuntarily searching my mind for the means to be even better off, but it was not wise for I am much happier than I could ever have hoped to be. But why is it, I wonder, that one is never content with one's fate? Tell me please, Father, you who know all, what pushes us to always desire something new as soon as we have the thing that we had wanted?"

"My friend, it is because we are seeking to fill the emptiness in our hearts but we can't do it because this little nook that is never filled is the place of God. It will never be occupied by anything of this world so that we will always have room to think of Him."

"Father, you are doing me a great favor to explain what has always tormented me. Now I'll be more contented. I'll work with even more pleasure and I'll bear my troubles with patience."

(Maurice tried to teach his old friend Frisé good work habits.)

"Are you not ashamed to receive charity when the good Lord gave you two strong arms solidly attached to your body? Why do neither you nor your children work?"

"To tell you the truth Maurice, when I see everybody busy and when I cannot find anyone in the whole village to talk to, I feel badly. I don't know why it is, but when I do feel like working I can't find a job. Besides, I never have been lucky!"

"Frisé, you must chase luck and I don't recall you ever trying to catch it."

"That's easy for you to say, Maurice; you have always had good luck."

"Ha! Ha! You think so! Well then, do you want me to tell you where I found my good luck so that you can find some too?"

"Yes, tell me about it! It wouldn't upset me to find it."

"First," Maurice continued, "I never go to a bar, for it is never found there."

"That is not to your credit, for you have plenty of wine in your house."

"I can show you that I don't spend any more than you do on wine, though everyone in my household drinks it."

"Tell me, I'm eager to hear how you do that!"

"Listen carefully! You drink at least three bottles a week in a bar, don't you?"

"Say four to be more correct and there'll still probably be one missing."

"All right, let's say four! A bottle costs you at least twenty-five centimes, which come to one franc."

"Add fifty more centimes for the friends who drink with me."

"One franc a week makes fifty-two francs in one year, all in all seventy-eight francs a year. With that much money, Frisé, you could buy three casks of Nohan wine for fifteen francs each, after you return the casks, and your wine won't be of bad quality. When you add the fees and shipping, you'll have eighteen francs, which makes fifty-four francs total and you can see that you have money left over. Look, Frisé, aren't three casks of wine plenty in houses such as ours?"

"Here! Here! I never thought to make those calculations! Now tell me about your good luck."

"Here is my good luck. While after a meal you take a nap, I hit hard on an anvil, and if you were not so soundly asleep at night you would hear me sometimes striking upon the iron after ten o'clock."

"Why do you stay so late if you work all day?"

"What for! To satisfy my clients, whom I never make wait; to work two hours more a day which makes six hundred extra working hours by the end of the year, and six hundred hours are worth fifty days. Charles, young though he is, often does as I do. That is my good luck, my friend, and anyone could have the same. While you always postpone what you have to do and never get it done, I am, on the contrary, always ahead as much as possible, for I never know what awaits me the next day and what might prevent me from keeping my word with my customers. You see, Frisé, my anvil never refuses to give me money if I ask for it with good hammer blows."

"That may be, but I would think your arms would ache by the end of the day."

"I won't say that they don't. It happens quite often, but when they hurt so much that I can't raise them, I go home to sit down for a few minutes and Françoise brings me a glass of wine! While I drink I let my eyes roam around the room which is so clean and so well furnished. I see my little ones well dressed and lively and my wife nursing the baby and singing, and I feel my fatigue disappear at once. Then I take up my hammer and I strike it well!"

"Oh well, I'm not like that. I don't like to be at home. When I have to go there and I see the rooms so cold and bare and the children in rags, I leave at once."

"Yes, and you go to the bar to forget the misery that you have created."

"Damn! It takes so much effort to get even the necessary things!"

"If we could find everything without any effort, Frisé, we would be worth nothing in the end. Need makes our head work and warms our heart. Every morning when I think of the means to feed my family and make them comfortable, I feel much better, honestly. How I do love them!"

"All that you say, Maurice, moves my soul. I feel like trying your kind of luck. You see, I don't want to tell anyone but you, for you have my confidence: when I spend all my money in the bar the bread of charity tastes bitter to me."

"And that of work tastes so good!"

"I want you to understand that I'm not used to working diligently any more. Maybe I'm not good enough to put forth a strenuous effort. Besides, who would want to give me work?"

"I will, Frisé. there is a corner of my garden where nothing grows because it is all stones. If you plough it, I'll give you a franc and twenty-five centimes a day; that amounts to seven francs and fifty centimes a week and there is enough work for a whole month. I know the value of money since I earn it by the sweat of my brow and I'm not in the mood to lose, so I'll watch you closely; thus, no bars any more. Does it suit you?"

"Yes, Maurice. I want to know if one is really content, as they all say, to bring the fruits of one's labor to the wife at the end of the week. But, do you realize that seven francs and fifty centimes is nothing to feed six people with?"

"And when you have no money to give them, it is even less! Do you think your people have what they want now when you bring nothing, so to speak, to them? Do you care at all for them? At this moment when the harvest has not started yet, good workers hardly make as much as I offer you. If you become reliable the money you'll be earning every Sunday, will soon make things comfortable. Well, have you made up your mind? It will be a good decision if you say yes. Besides, when you feel that you are losing heart, go to see the priest. He will quickly build you up again when he explains to you that God created us to work, and also he loves you and the affection of a man like the priest, Frisé, will give you the strength to do the impossible! Understand?"

"All right. I absolutely want to give it a try."

Frisé became a good worker and his wife and children also improved.

The next year at the carnival Frisé came in his finest clothes to ask

Maurice, his father-in-law, and Charles to come to supper with him on Shrove Sunday.

"Frisé, I don't want you to spend your money on us. Therefore, no supper."

"You cannot refuse me that pleasure, Maurice, for it is not good if you only oblige people. You still have to respect them. Without that, you see, it would be too difficult to accept one's favors. If you don't come to have supper with us they will say that you despise me and it will hurt my reputation in this region, to say nothing of the mortal pain it will bring to me. My wife has stuffed two of her goslings to serve you and you must come to eat them."

"You are right, Frisé. We'll come to have supper with you. Count on us."

On Sunday, Maurice, on coming into Frisé's house where he had not been for a very long time, found the house clean and orderly. The place settings were on the table, his wife well dressed, and the children too. They all came for the purpose of having supper with the blacksmith.

"Now I am happy like you, Maurice, though I am not rich. Our children are content in service and they behave well and are in good health. The little one goes to school and he is so clean that it is a pleasure to look at him. I work all week without wasting a single day. And my wife spins for yours when she can find no work outside our house. Now! Are you satisfied? For it is you who worked this miracle!"

"Not I alone, Frisé! I think the priest also has something to do with this."

"That is true. Without him I could very well fall back into my habitual laziness, for at times I found it rough to get up before dawn to go thresh the whole day long. When my arms hurt, I thought that it was also that way with you and that it did not stop you, even though you are not in need, and if I still did not have the heart to work I went to see the priest and he raised my spirits. After that I returned to work with pleasure. Eventually, I got into the habit so well that I truly think if I were paid to loaf, as I used to do, I would not enjoy it."

"Did I not tell you, my Frisé, that you would find happiness in work? Wait a few more years! When you are able to buy one or two parcels of land with your money you'll see what joy it is to work on it! For what is acquired with so much effort is much appreciated I'm telling you!"

"What you have said is so true, Maurice! I'm wearing a shirt made of hemp that I sowed and which my wife gathered, crushed, combed and spun, and it feels soft as silk. Oh God! How many kinds of satisfaction I was never aware of! Children, come thank this man. Without him you would have become delinquents, and you would more and more despise your father, who allowed you to drink nothing but water while he was getting drunk in the tavern. As you can see, Maurice, now there is enough wine here for everyone and I drink only my share."

Maurice embraced them all and went home happy with Frisé's conversion which had made him an excellent worker.

(Charles, Maurice's son, discussed freedom of choice with a stranger.)

"You are talking about the soul, young man, as though you understand what it is. Do you know whether we have the freedom to govern it and if we are able to control our thoughts?"

"Oh, yes, Monsieur! The teacher explained all that to me very well."

"Tell us, then, how you interpret what he had to say."

"First of all, he pointed out to me that we are not always masters of our thoughts and quite often we have bad ones against our will. For example, envy will make us desire what belongs to another, though we are honest in our hearts. On the other hand, we are not in control either when we think well of what, in fact, is wrong. When we find an ugly thing beautiful or an injustice to be fair. That knowledge was in our soul when God gave it to us. He gave us the freedom to do well according to our conscience, or to do evil when we become the victims of our own fantasy. Thus, it depends absolutely upon ourselves if we don't listen to our conscience. One only has to have a strong character and to pray to God for Him to come to our assistance."

Years passed and Maurice lived in growing prosperity, for the comforts he had achieved only increased his love of work and he was perfectly happy. Charles was twenty years old and was thinking about the draft. He matured early. When he was young there was concern that he would not be able to withstand the fatigue of military service, but, on the contrary, he was strong and well built. Eventually his number was drawn and, despite his mother's despair, it was decided that he should go before the roll call so that he could be placed in the special troops.

"My child, you should try to enter as a blacksmith in an artillery regiment. I served under the command of the recruitment captain in Chateauroux when he was only a lieutenant, and he has always been benevolent towards me. I'll give you a letter for him and I'm sure he'll arrange everything to the best of your advantage." And in fact, that captain enrolled Charles in the second artillery regiment which was garrisoned in Bescançon.

Having told his family good-by, Charles reported to that city. When he arrived he had to take a short exam and, since he was able to prove his ability, he was made a monitor at the regimental school. At the same time, while teaching reading, writing and arithmetic, he was learning geometrical drawing and some advanced mathematics. His ability and good nature were noticed by his superiors and they came to rely on him.

(M. Berthaud, who was in charge of the farm belonging to the mansion, asked Maruice,) "How did it happen that you didn't settle down in a town? It seems to me that you would get bored in this village."

"Why so, Monsieur?"

"Because you are so much more educated than the people around you."

"M. Berthaud, the simplest of my neighbors knows many things that are unknown to me and I have never met anyone, not even among the women who do night work with us, who could not have taught me something."

"I suppose that is possible, but you give a hundred times more than you get in return from others."

"Not true, Monsieur! Every time the priest, the teacher, all of you messieurs, come to talk to me, you give to me and I learn something. Isn't it only fair that I return what you give to me so generously? Had they had the opportunity to go to school and had they been in the army as I was and lived in such close friendship with the priest and our teacher, perhaps they would be worth more than I am."

"I doubt that, Maurice," M. Berthaud said, "but how is it that only half of the children who could go to school, do, in fact, go there? If the women in this country had regularly attended school they would be able to bring up their families and take care of them with more intelligence. They would get more work done and do it better. Houses would be cleaner and, therefore, healthier. Why, in ten years it would no longer be possible to recognize your village, so much would change."

"So, you think just as I do, M. Berthaud! However, when I try to explain it to the women of the village they say that if one has so many things on one's mind, one is no good for any one thing."

"What a ridiculous idea! It is the same with the men who incur debts in order to buy land, no matter what the price. Would it not be more wise for them to save some money and improve the fields they already own instead of living close to poverty and misery. If they took from their savings, they would not have to sell their grain when the price is low in order to survive and could hold off till the prices go up. Then they could even increase their savings, but they are as stubborn as their wives and many years will pass before this area becomes as civilized as some other parts of France. It's not worth discussing any more."

"Why not? Do talk, M. Berthaud, do talk! It is never a waste to repeat worthwhile advice. To give them an example of what you say, do like our good priest, who throws a thousand words to the wind just to have a single word or idea picked up and bring fruit. He knows well, the saintly man, that one has to say something often and continue to repeat good ideas before they will develop in those thick heads full of pride and ignorance. They don't want to know how much the times have changed and that the person who was able to do business in the past without being able to read and write could not do so today."

At that moment a man who was briskly driving a cart, pulled by two beautiful horses, entered Maurice's yard. "Do you have ready-made shoes for these animals?" he asked. "I'm going to town and I'll return in three hours. I'd prefer not to have to wait very long."

"Yes, master Robin, I have what you need and I'll take care of you at once. You move very fast, old man! I remember that you did not move at such a pace about ten years ago!"

"Ah well, one has to keep up with the times. My deceased father would not make his cart-horse trot even if his life depended on it. He was certain it would ruin the horse and I thought the same, but eventually, I saw that if I went on walking everybody would soon pass me by and I couldn't accomplish as much business. I've already started to feel it."

"I believe you, for in the end our wealth is the result of our work efforts and the more one works, the wealthier one becomes."

"And, since the greatest instrument of work is time," M. Berthaud added, "the person who knows how not to waste it has the advantage."

"What you say is absolutely true, Monsieur, and we don't give it enough serious thought. I know a lot of people who like to work, but, in spite of that, live poorly because they don't know how to use their time properly. This exposes them to many deprivations, while arranging their work better would allow them to save more and live better."

One day while Françoise and her daughter were very busy folding the freshly washed linen and Françoise's father was reading to them *The Life of Saint François De Sales,* Maurice came in with a letter in his hand and shouted, "Rejoice! Charles is coming home and won't be leaving any more!" At those words, they all embraced each other, crying from joy.

"Read this letter to us quickly, Maurice," the old blacksmith said, "so that I can see whether the boy still remembers his grandfather."

"Then listen: 'My dear and kind parents, The regiment is leaving Besançon and moving to Vincennes, near Paris, and for this reason discharge was issued to all men who had less than a year of service left. When my turn came, my captain told me that I was wrong to leave the corps, for I would soon become an officer or an artillery guard, if that is what I preferred, and that such a position was worth more than that of the village blacksmith. I refused all of his offers, following your example, my dear father! Like you, despite all the advantages I was offered at the regiment, I prefer to rely upon the work of my own hands, among those whom I love. They tried everything in order to convince me. Everyone tried, even the colonel, which does me great honor, but I resisted bravely and in less than two weeks I'll embrace you all. So, be happy, as I am, and let us forget this long absence which hurt my good mother and my grandfather so much. Was I not right to say he would drink at my wedding because, dear father, I sincerely hope that the Michands have not forgotten me.

Adieu, and see you soon. I embrace you with all my heart. With respect and affection, Your son, Charles Ferragu.' "

CHAPTER EIGHT

Old Age

Jeanne was widowed early and Nannette went into service at the Dumont's to help her mother meet expenses. Nannette was like Jeanne in every way. She soon married a young man who took over the management of Jeanne's farm. Jeanne lived on with her daughter and son-in-law and in her old age enjoyed her grand-children. Her world remained bounded by home and family.

Maurice also saw his children prospering, his son following in his footsteps. Charles only regretted that he wouldn't be able to say that he owed his fortune solely to his own work, a fact of which Maurice was so proud. Unlike Jeanne, Maurice also took on major roles outside of home and family. He became an assistant mayor and through his leadership major improvements in the village roads were completed. Thus, in old age Maurice continued the pattern established earlier, of turning to achievements in the outer world and valuing himself for them.

Jeanne, Widow

(The priest urged Jeanne to pray to accept her husband's death since it was God's will.)

Jeanne had a little boy whom she named after his father. Mme. Isaure wanted to be his godmother.

One day she came to see her godson and found him quite weak. "Jeanne, if you were wise you would wean Louis. Your milk has gone bad because of your great sorrow and you are doing this child a great deal of harm."

Jeanne followed the advice and the child recovered initially, but soon after became ill again.

(The priest told Jeanne that he wanted to place her eldest son, Sylvain, with a notary in town. Jeanne would have preferred him to remain a peasant like his father, "For this is the position which makes one most contented and which causes the least harm to others." But, she prepared his clothes and the priest took him to town.)

Louis had turned three years old. He recovered his good health and became very strong. He spoke very little and what he did say was quite different from ordinary children's talk. He ran after every shiny object he saw, trying to catch it. Several times he burned himself with a candle, pulled logs out of the fire to play with them, and finally, one day threw himself into the creek to pick up the sun he saw reflected in the water. Neither his mother nor his sister ever left him alone, fearing an accident. Jeanne said to the child's godmother, "I can't be mistaken, Madame; my poor Louis will be simple-minded all his life, even if he does not turn out to be a complete idiot. I cannot possibly be mistaken, for this is not the first time I have seen a simple-minded child. He'll be a child of God all his life and I won't be able to leave him for a moment."

"Then, Jeanne, if you cannot work because of Louis, give me Nannette. I'll take care of her as if she were my own daughter. You won't need to spend anything for her food. On the contrary, she'll be able to help you with what she will earn at my house."

"Thank you, my dear lady. It will be difficult for us to separate, for she loves my Louis almost more than I, but it's too much to have two women in a house and I'll be happy to know that she is with you."

No sooner had Mme. Isaure gone, than Nannette, who was crying in the other room because she had heard everything, began to exclaim, "My dear mother, we are to be separated! I'll never be able to stand it! I'll die!"

"My poor girl, you won't die because of that. When I lost your father I did not die because I thought about you, my children, and you'll think about me to gain more courage."

"But it will be so difficult to live with strangers!"

"Naturally it is better to live with one's parents when it is possible. Our misfortune makes it necessary for us to separate, my Nannette, but it won't be forever. There are just too many mouths to feed here and also I am not able to buy you any clothes. Now, all that you earn will be yours, my daughter."

"And yours too, my dear mother, but I won't be able to live without seeing you."

"You will, my girl. You'll have a lot of work and you won't have time to think so much about us. Mme. Isaure is very kind. She won't be an ordinary mistress to you. It was she who gave me the first money in my life, who taught me everything I know. She always protected me. You'll feel better with her than here with me and you will soon grow to love her, I'm sure of it!"

But Nannette would not be soothed. Her mother told her, "My child, go to see the priest. He has the right words for every sorrow and you will pray to God with him."

The priest had Nannette stay for supper with him and brought her home afterwards.

"Isn't she lucky," Jeanne said, "in our great misfortune to find a place so close by and with people we love so much?"

"Yes, Jeanne, and she understands that now. I promise you she'll be more sensible about it now."

"Nannette, we'll go tomorrow to Mme. Dumont's to ask when they will be needing you. If your eyes are swollen from crying she'll think that you've forgotten everything she's done for us."

"Mother, I'll take your cow to the fields now, it will help me to calm down."

(Nannette began to work for Mme. Isaure. Sylvain had one week of leave time in the spring and came back home. He brought money to help his mother. Paul, the second son, did not want to work in the fields. He wanted to be a blacksmith and go on the Tour de France. Jeanne decided to let him work in father Maurice's shop.)

Sometime after that Solange came to see Jeanne and told her, "Would you like to give your daughter to my Jean? Since he returned from the army he thinks of no one but her. He says there is no other girl like her and if she refuses him, he won't ever marry."

"Solange, we have to ask Nannette first what she has to say."

"Maybe she won't want to stay in the country now that she has tried town living."

"You are mistaken, Solange. I know she will be happy only if she lives with me and that she will only accept a man who will agree to live in our house and work our land."

"Wonderful! This is what Jean wants also."

"This is not all, Solange. There is my little Louis who may very well annoy your son. Nannette loves him as much as I do. If Jean cannot endure him she will be unhappy and I'll have to leave, for there is nothing in the whole world that will force me to part with my poor son."

"Your little Louis is as strong as four men and my son likes him. He says that simple ones are closer to God than others. Just this morning he said he would show him how to plough and he is sure he'll be able to do it, so don't worry about that."

"Well then! Since we agree, go to Mme. Dumont's and tell Nannette that I have to talk to her and we'll find out at once what she thinks about it."

When Nannette arrived, her mother told her, "My girl, maîtresse Jusserand came to ask you for her son."

"Yes, my little Nannette," Solange said, "would you like to take a peasant for a husband now that you are almost a young lady?"

"Mother, I'll marry only if I stay with you."

"My girl, Jean Jusserand agrees to live in our house and cultivate our land, but you should not think about me in such an important decision. I want you to tell me if you like him."

"Yes, mother," Nannette said, blushing, "Jean is nicer and more learned than other boys in our village, but I dare not tell Madame, who is so good to me and whom I love so much, that I'm going to leave her."

"I'll go with you, don't worry."

"Come and kiss me, my Nannette," Solange said, "you can't imagine how happy I'll be to call you my daughter-in-law, I, who owe everything to your mother!"

(Jeanne told Mme. Isaure of her plans for Nannette.)

"Madame, it's not easy for me to tell you what is happening, though I'm sure you won't become angry. Nannette has found a good match. It is time for her to get married and I think it would be wrong to refuse."

"What, Jeanne, you want to take away Nannette, whom I trust completely like a daughter?"

"Madame, Nannette will never find another boy like Jean Jusserand. He is rich, good-natured, and is better educated than other peasant boys. Very simply put, he has everything! Then too, he wants to live with us and cultivate our land and I am sure he'll never bully this poor creature who sleeps at your feet," she gestured.

"It seems to me, Jeanne, that in your place I'd like something better for Nannette. She does not seem to be born to live in the country. I thought that one day she would marry a good worker from the town."

"Madame," Nannette said, "I know only two houses where I can live, yours and my mother's. Had I not found a man who wanted to live with my mother I would have never left your service."

"Then too, Madame," Jeanne said, "one is more content working one's own land than working for customers who can always go away and leave without paying; while the farmer, obliged to God alone, never grumbles, believe me."

"Well, Nannette, get married then since you want it so, but I'll still need you quite often."

"Madame, my mother will take care of the house and I'll be able to go out to work and I'll be happy whenever you, Madame, would like to hire me."

Within a short time, Nannette married. Sylvain arrived for the ceremony. He looked quite cosmopolitan but he did not make a show of it and it was easy to see that he was happy to be with his family again and also with his good neighbors. But all of that did not comfort Jeanne, who would have preferred to see him a farmer.

(Jeanne wanted to divide her property among her children and live on a pension from them. Sylvain explained the disadvantages of such a decision. On the contrary, they all wanted to support Louis and Jean, who was taking care of him, but the formalities could not be arranged without Paul.)

Three years after Nannette's marriage, at the beginning of March, Jeanne was sitting on the balcony watching Louis plough on the other side of the road; he was ploughing with more care and intelligence than one could have expected from him. Jeanne was so deeply immersed in her thoughts that she did not hear footsteps on the staircase and then, raising her eyes to some motion in the air, she saw a full-grown boy beside her. She was so struck when she recognized Paul that she could only open her arms to embrace him without a word spoken. They cried together in silence. Paul finally arose while his mother gazed at him with pride, such a handsome boy he had become.

"Wicked child," she said, hugging him again, "to leave us all these years without any news! Why did you not write?"

"I did not want to write to you before I had become worthy of you."

For supper the whole family congregated to celebrate Paul's arrival. Nannette cooked a better meal than usual, while Jean brought out the good wine; and they all sat down for the feast.

(Paul told how he spent his time after he left the blacksmith's shop; working on a road gang, eating only bread and water. Eventually he began to understand all that his mother had taught him. After a time he resumed his Tour de France.)

Paul wrote immediately to Sylvain, who came over with a form showing that he and Paul had given their rights of legacy to their sister, Nannette, with the life-interest going to their mother, and to Louis after her death.

Jeanne could finally live in peace. Her daughter became mistress of the house while she, herself, took any work she could find. For half the year she was employed at Mme. Dumont's.

Paul settled in the town where, several years later, he bought a shop and married Louise's daughter. Jeanne, in her old age, was as happy as she could possibly be, seeing all of her children well off and held in great esteem. She grew old among her family and died, lamented by all, but most of all by her children, who never forgot her.

Maurice — Assistant Mayor

(Maurice married off his son and daughter on the same day. Charles married his second cousin and Clementine married the son of Maurice's best friend, Cordier.)

The marriages took place at Maurice's home. Clementine went to live with her mother-in-law, and Charles, while waiting for his house to be finished, stayed in his grandfather's room and the old man told everybody, "Now I don't worry anymore! I am sure that Charles will be here to close my eyes when I pass on."

On the eve of the weddings Maurice said to his son in the presence of the future father-in-law, "Charles, we should make our financial agreements before you get married so that everything will be in order."

"Father, it won't take us long because I want to work with you. You'll give me what you find proper. I am sure I'll be well paid for my work."

"My child, I'll pay you on the same scale as a hard worker and, having your house and the field that I'm giving you, you won't be looked down on. Besides, you will inherit from me one day and you will be certain to have a good house, so long as you live in an acceptable manner."

(Charles said that he could never be as happy as Maurice.)

"Why is that, my dear child?"

"Because I won't have earned it myself, as you did, and I can't love every stone of it as you do, for they won't remind me of my own efforts or difficulties. I won't be able to tell myself, 'It is I who, with God's help, created all this from the fruits of my labor. I am the only creator of my wife's and my children's prosperity.' Look, father, no other satisfaction can ever come close to that!"

"It's true, my child, but there is sometimes as much reward in preserving one's well-being as in creating a small fortune by yourself. Look, rather, at what happened to poor Bertrand! Besides, do you think I did not have my troubles?"

"I know very well, father, that it was not all roses for you, but you defeated the bad luck by your persevering work and, while helping your neighbors all the time, you achieved an independent position; and that is true satisfaction!"

"Maurice," M. Lenoir said. "we're going to reappoint one half of the municipal council staff along with the mayor and his assistant. The prefect asked me whether I'd like to stay on in the town hall. I gave him an affirmative answer, but on the condition that you will be my assistant. Will you accept such an appointment?"

"Monsieur, you do me a great honor but it will be difficult for me to accept. First of all, I have to work. Then, it seems to me that M. Berthaud, your farmer, is much more capable of helping you than I am."

"My dear Maurice, M. Berthaud, in spite of his intelligence and fine qualities, won't be as useful to the community as you because he is a stranger in this region and will never have much influence on the inhabitants. As for the type of work, I'm certain you wouldn't be reluctant to take several hours away from home to devote to the well-being of your compatriots!"

"M. Lenoir is right, Maurice," the wheelwright said, "for a long time we have not had a capable deputy and the community suffers during the absences of Monsieur, who passes all of his winters in Bourges."

"There, Maurice," M. Lenoir insisted, "don't refuse me. Between the two of us we'll change the face of this land. We'll clean the streets of the village; they are so muddy that it disgraces the whole village. I am prepared to do all that you ask of me and, in your position, you know much better than I how to stimulate the harmony of the inhabitants."

"Very well, Monsieur Lenoir, since you want it so much I won't refuse to become your deputy if I am appointed."

Soon after that, Maurice was appointed as deputy. It was the period of time when the annual road taxes were being determined. Maurice went to visit the mayor and told him, "Monsieur, our local roads are in such bad repair that quite soon it will no longer be possible to get to town, and at this point it will take several days to repair them. I have been to see all those who pay road taxes and they agree with me to pay the taxes with work rather than give money which ends up everywhere but here, since it is the privilege of the administration to do so. As soon as the notice is given, I'll activate the task force and, if you would like to do some supervising, I feel we will finally have the job done well."

M. Lenoir willingly agreed to go, like Maurice, to the site to supervise the taxpayers and oversee their work. They began with repairing the worst parts, but the road-tax work assignments were all paid off before they reached the interior of the village and Maurice was very disappointed.

One Sunday, after the mass, the men got together under a ledge and discussed business. Maurice spoke with them for a while and then, pointing to the church square which had many holes on it and which were filled with rain water, he said, "And are you not ashamed of this, to see your square in such a state of disrepair?"

"Well, yes," the innkeeper said; he was also the municipal counselor, "we'll have to flatten it out next year."

"And why not this year?"

"Because the money is depleted."

"Yes, the taxes were sent to the department, but what prevents us from imposing a work duty upon ourselves?"

"And our work! Who will do it if we give our time to fixing the streets of the village?"

"My God, we have the resources to do it all. I'm asking only for your wasted time and everyone knows that there are hours, and even half days, that we accomplish nothing because the weather does not allow us to go far from home. Give this wasted time to me and you will see!"

"I think we won't get much accomplished with those quarters of days," they all said, laughing.

"So, that is what you think! Well then, you are mistaken. Listen to what I have to say," Maurice continued. "In the village we have at least eighty laborers and thirty horses. Let everyone give me a quarter of a day a month! Is that asking too much?"

"No," they all answered together.

"Since a quarter out of eighty is twenty, I'll then have twenty days from the men and seven from the horses each month. With that, my friends, I expect to have streets as clean and smooth as the rows of a garden. Won't you be happy not to see your poor little ones in mud up to their knees?"

"Then give the command, Maurice, we are ready to do what you ask."

(Julien Blanchard, Maurice's old friend from Paris, visited him. Julien had bought property near Maurice and became his neighbor. His mother, Mme. Blanchard, now a widow, was with him also. His son, Paul, who had studied all the new agricultural methods, had come to improve the farming in the countryside. Maurice was delighted with their arrival. M. Lenoir asked Maurice to replace him as mayor. Maurice replied,)

"Me Monsieur! The town hall is too well off in your hands to pass it on to someone else."

"My friend, I cannot remain mayor any longer. The government calls me to other duties and no one but you is qualified to replace me here."

"Monsieur, I feel quite comfortable as second in command. It would be wrong to place myself in charge because I don't understand public administration well enough. Besides, I'm already old and the young must take their turn. They are active and know how to get things accomplished."

"But whom do you want us to choose as mayor among the young men in our district?"

"Since you ask my opinion, I think you can't do better than to ask Paul Blanchard. There he is, with a better education than anyone in the village. By going off to farming school his mind has developed more than the others."

"But, M. Blanchard is a stranger to this area. If he is asked to be mayor, you must make it possible for him to do all that one has a right to expect from a man such as he. You must promise me, my dear Maurice, that you will remain a deputy for a long time."

"I do promise you, Monsieur, and you can depend on me to do all that I can to be helpful to the community, and also to my friend's son."

As they were leaving the chateau, Julien grasped Maurice's hand tenderly, and told him, "My dear friend, you don't know what pleasure you have given me. My greatest dream was to see my son governing his community, but I was far from the hope that it would happen so soon. You have just made my dream become a reality!"

As he had promised, Paul fulfilled his duties as mayor with zeal and with fairness. If it was necessary to sacrifice one thing for another to make a particular improvement, he generously gave of himself, as did Maurice, who lived on to old age without any weaknesses or major problems that might have ruined his well-deserved happiness.

PART THREE

The Impact of Education on French Children

CHAPTER NINE

The Children Speak

The models Carraud presented to her readers exhibited a delicate balance between tradition and change. They sought to bring peasant children into the modern world with regard to the acceptance of two new ideas, progress and plannning, as well as two less abstract changes, literacy and improved standards of cleanliness. These new ideas and standards were wrapped in a cloak of traditional verities—hard work and good living, acceptance of religion and honoring one's elders, as well as remaining within the village community. For girls, there was a special emphasis on their role as mother and helpmate. Their main function remained "duty." For boys, the emphasis was on being the breadwinner, but their work took on the new dimension of self-fulfillment. For both, hard work was the essential ingredient of life, and for both there were skills which were learned from people other than their parents.[1] Maurice went on the *Tour de France* to learn new skills and Jeanne learned from Isaure skills that neither her mother nor Mère Nannette could teach her.

Both Jeanne and Maurice saw rewards for their efforts; Jeanne saw her children stay healthy and become respected in the community, while Maurice saw his business prosper. Both Maurice and Jeanne were taught that work was necessary to live, but they gradually translated this message into the more modern idea—time is money. Simultaneously, the division of labor according to gender became more pronounced: boys learned skills that earned money while girls perfected "woman's work"—child care and household skills. Increasingly, women's world was restricted to the home and men's to the outside world. Consequently, Maurice's world, the world of men, was open to continuous change while Jeanne's world, having adopted new standards of cleanliness and child care, became immutable and took on the mantle of being "natural." The evidence for this was most clear in young Nannette's desire to become just like her mother, while Jeanne's sons continued their education and each son took up jobs different from the agricultural labor performed by Grand Louis.

The historian attempting to use Carraud's *Jeanne* and *Maurice*, as well as other school books and pedagogical manuals as sources in the study of gender attitude formation, must inevitably ask how much of the bourgeois message was assimilated by rural children in the nineteenth century. This question is essentially one of the transference of a set of ideas held by one group to another group with different economic and social circumstances. Thomas Laquer has argued that the bourgeois world view triumphed in England largely through consent, not through force. The middle classes achieved a moral hegemony; their concept of reality "diffused throughout society in all its institutional and private manifestations, informing with its spirit all taste, morality, customs, religious and political principles, and all social relations, particularly in their intellectual and moral connotations." [2]

Can we say the same for France? Did customs and social relations change in the Haute Garonne, the Loire, the Cher? It is clear that school books frequently expressed values which were at variance with those of the children who were being taught them.[3] One might almost conclude a negative correlation between values taught and those held by the newcomers to the school (otherwise there would be no compulsion to keep reiterating them). Indeed, in one example of a school reader, *Les Récréations de l'école*, Mme. A. J. T. Pinet, the author, introduced a dialogue in which a pupil questioned her teacher's views:

Mme. Louise: . . and however young you are, you will appreciate the true and profound sense of these words: "Pity the children who lacked the tenderness and care of a family and in whom the heart did not learn to beat near other hearts. God wanted downy creatures (babies) to

be in all the nests. The young bird needs to feel protected in this soft refuge, under its mother's wing. That doesn't stop it from flying off one day, strong, powerful, capable of great flight through tempests."
Marie: That's good for the mothers who have a certain degree of comfort and have nothing else to do but coddle their children all the time: our mothers, daughters of workers, have other things to think about: They have to feed their families before they take time out to cover them with caresses.
Mme. Louise: It is possible to have nests and downy ones in the most humble of households. It is another form of Christian equality that we find all over and of which the family is the most complete example. As with the material goods that are most necessary and best—the sun, the air, and rushing water, which are at the service of the whole world—so the most excellent moral goods are offered to all: religion and the family. You can't buy a family at the market or the Stock Exchange: one hasn't more because one is rich, or less because one is poor. God did not permit such privileges. Instruction varies according to our resources; education does not vary.[4]

But did Marie assimilate this lesson? My hunch is that the goal of establishing a "downy nest" was adapted to Marie's views of what such a nest would look like. Further, Marie's life experience, governed by her ideas of what was appropriate and also by the economic and social relations she entered, gradually shaped her view of that nest. Marie's daughter, in turn, would have a different view of the nest she wished to establish, but probably would not question the goal of making one.

A study of women's attitudes about childrearing in Picardy, done in the 1960s, lends credence to my thesis. An analysis of the habits of two sisters, daughters of a peasant/day laborer, revealed that one daughter remained traditional, while the other modernized. Interviews with the sisters are summarized in table 6.[5]

When questioned about why she was different from her sister, the modern sister answered, "I learned new customs in school and from the family I worked for when I left school." The traditional sister explained that she learned how to raise children from her mother; since she was the eldest daughter she had to help out a lot at home. Divergence within families points out that sisters, and certainly peers, may react differently to similar stimuli. The fact of having been exposed to new ideas—in school for example—does not necessarily imply that these ideas are accepted. One must make

TABLE 6

Modern Sister	*Traditional Sister*
1. She attended school through the age of fourteen and passed her Certificate of Studies exam.	1. She quit school at thirteen and did not take her final exam.
2. She married a factory worker and had four children.	2. She married a mason, who drank and was a known wife abuser. They had seven children.
3. Her husband built a house of six rooms. She kept everything orderly.	3. They lived in two rooms. The boys slept on straw in an attic. The house was always disorderly.
4. When she left for work at 8:30, the housework was complete.	4. She had no steady employment.
5. She felt her family was upwardly mobile.	5. She had no feelings concerning mobility.
6. Her eldest son went to a technical college.	6. She had no plans for her children's education.
7. She did not nurse her children, nursing was too time-consuming and old-fashioned.	7. She nursed all seven of her children because she thought it better and also cheaper.
8. She had three bottles and sterilized them. The babies were fed on a regular schedule.	8. She thought that in order to nurse well she had to eat a lot and drink plenty of beer. She prepared heavy foods. She only had one bottle which she only rinsed with clear water. She fed her babies on demand.
9. She charted the growth of her children.	9. She had no scale. Sometimes she took the babies to the hospital to be weighed.
10. Her children were toilet-trained between 12 and 14 months.	10. Her children were trained at the age of three when they had to go to school.
11. She never rocked her babies.	11. She frequently rocked her babies to sleep.

some effort to integrate new ideas into a preexisting culture.[6] A sampling of nineteenth-century pupils' notebooks shows how some accepted new ideas, and others rejected them.[7]

Eugénie Marin was born in Malesherbes (in the Loiret) on September 17, 1862. She attended a neighborhood primary school and later entered a religious boarding school. In 1875, she was asked to write a composition in the form of a letter home. She wrote:

Dear Mother,

It was with great joy that I returned here to our dear little pension which I left with so much happiness at the beginning of the vacation. I was so happy to see the beloved seats in the classroom, especially thinking about how I am going to sit there with all my little friends whom I was so happy to see after such a long absence. Also, dear Mother, in the midst of my happiness I made some good resolutions: to improve my learning, never to disobey my teachers, and to be very sweet and good to all my friends. I feel very much full of good will to do everything I am told, especially to try very hard this year to make my work very good so that you will see a well-instructed daughter return to you.

Good-bye, dear Mother. Think about all the good resolutions and be sure that I love you with all my heart. Your obedient daughter,

E. Marin.

Eugénie's composition clearly reflected the image of the dutiful child prevalent in school literature of the nineteenth century. T. H. Barrau's advice to children was representative of the literature which emphasized filial duty, in a period marked by rapid social change. Barrau wrote: "It is not only during youth that children must respect parents, but for our entire lives. Not only we, but our spouses and children must respect our parents. If we become more learned or more wealthy, we shouldn't get proud and think of ourselves as superior. It is better to remain ignorant and poor than to be ungrateful." [8]

Eugénie Marin wrote a second composition in 1875, which showed that she had accepted Barrau's ideas of filial duty and the special role of the dutiful daughter. The composition is entitled, "The Good Heart of a Little Girl":

At the Bureau of the Mont de Piété (state pawnshop), about six o'clock in the morning, many poor people were already gathered to present themselves to the clerk. Among them, there was a pretty little girl who seemed to wait impatiently for her turn. Finally, she approached the booth and put her little package on the counter. The clerk opened it and took out a doll. He asked, "What do you want me to do with this, my little child?" The little girl replied in a soft and sincere voice that her father was sick and her mother was crying and there was no food left and she had just decided to bring her doll. The clerk hid a tear and withdrew behind the counter, apparently to estimate the value of the doll. He came back a few moments later holding in his hands the doll and a five-franc piece which he gave to the girl saying, "Here, this is for your doll."

Eugénie Marin, clearly, was receptive to the ideas current in the schools of the 1860s and '70s. T. H. Barrau's Mlle. Josserand and Elizabeth Loupouloff, as well as A. E. de Saintes' Laure, were heroines of school literature who could well have been models for Eugénie's composition. Not only were daughters to be obedient, but they were to share a secret understanding with their mothers, as in this poignant scene from "Mlle. Josserand": [9]

Her mother, her poor mother, was there dying . . . Her daughter, coming near to her, understood the wishes which the mother held in her heart without daring to express them, and she devoted herself to fulfilling them. Working day and night and scrimping would enable her to pay off the family's debts.

Not all of the children's notebooks showed receptivity to these modern ideas. Louis Massot, writing in 1890 in Elbeuf, clearly refused to become "civilized." In the beginning of his notebook, we find a handwriting exercise in which Louis copied: "It is important to be orderly. Your clothing should be kept neat; your books and your notebooks too. All these objects cost a lot of money and the money is earned with great difficulty by your father." Louis' work was not neat and his teacher commented: "Many mistakes." The teacher gave him a grade of 4½ (out of a possible 10). Later on, he was asked to write a composition on the same subject. This time the teacher gave him a grade of 3 and commented: "No ideas."

But it is difficult to believe that Louis was ignorant. On the math and grammar assignments he scored 6½ and 10. It is likely that he simply refused to accept the ideas being offered him and, therefore, wrote poorly and very little. In one final example from Massot's notebook, he was asked to finish a story about two boys, Edmond and Eugène, playing marbles: Edmond wom many times and Eugène, in frustration, began to hit his opponent. Massot, clearly disinterested in the answer that the teacher would have liked to have (see below, work by Gaston Bigot), simply wrote: "Edmond went to look for another playmate with whom he will have more fun." Again the teacher wrote "No ideas."

Louis Massot refused to accept the new behavior advocated by both school books and teachers. Another similar case of spontaneous rejection of modern ideas can be found in a remarkable composition of unknown date and place (c. 1900, Corrèze). In this case, the pupil was asked to write about one of his friends who was frequently tardy and how that inconvenienced the whole class. The student started the composition as if reciting a formula:

> The teacher was in the middle of teaching us the fable, the "Carpe et les carpillons," when suddenly in the middle of the recitation the door opened and André entered. The teacher stopped to ask André why he was late. André said, "I had to feed the cows." The teacher exclaimed, "Yesterday you said you overslept, today it's the cows' fault, every day you have an excuse!" The teacher punished André, and the lesson had to be started all over again.

The pupil, however, could not control his real thoughts about this lesson and added one final sentence: *"Il faut travailler car le travaille est la mère de tous vices"* ("One must work because work is the mother of all vice"). The teacher crossed out the latter part of the sentence in red ink.

Teachers in the primary schools of the last century were not likely to give up on a child they considered capable of learning the new ideology. The notebooks of Cyr Bigot and his son, Gaston, are illustrative of the increasing control of new ideas on succeeding generations of children. Cyr Bigot was born in 1856 in the village of Saint Prest, situated seven kilometers north of Chartres, depart ment of Eure. There, he started out as a very poor pupil in the class of M. Friteau, a graduate of the normal school of Chartres. Cyr was still illiterate at the age of ten. But Friteau was convinced that the boy was educable and convinced his parents to allow him to stay in school one more year. Cyr's notebooks suddenly showed vast im- provement and in three years he received a diploma signed by the

Composition française

Un de vos camarades a la mauvaise habitude
d'arriver en retard à l'école. Décrivez son entrée
en classe. Indiquez quels inconvénients cette
facheuse habitude a pour votre camarade et
pour la classe entière.

Développement

Ce matin un de nos camarades est arrivé en
retard.

Le maître était entrain de nous apprendre
la fable de la carpe et les carpillons, le maître
a commencé de à nous la récité pour nous
apprendre comment il faut dire.

Tout a-coup au milieu de la récitation on
entend la porte s'ouvrir c'était André qui
arrive. Le maître le fait passer au piquet
et lui dit pourquoi arrive-tu en retard.
Monsieur il m'a fallu donné a mes vaches.
Hier matin tu m'a dit que tu était levé en
retard, aujourd'hui il a fallu donné à tes
vaches, tous les jours tu a quelques choses à me dire
André passe a sa place en regardant la
punition que le maître lui inscrit sur le tableau
Il place sa serviette et croise les bras.
Le maître avait déjà dit la moitié de récitation
il fallut recommencea pour André.
Il faut travailler car le travaille est la
~~richesse toujours~~.

17. Composition Française

prefect in recognition of his high merit. This diploma, because it carried the prefect's seal, was highly valued in the village. It was hung in the Bigot home next to the portrait of Pope Pius IX.

Cyr went to attend the Ecole Normale in Chartres from 1872 to 1875 and then was appointed as a teacher in Combres; later he became the director of a larger school in Janville; from there he moved on to Chateaudun and, finally, Chartres. In 1882, Gaston was born. He became his father's pupil in 1893 in Chateaudun. Remembering that Cyr was still illiterate at the age of ten, it is remarkable to read the composition of his son written at about the same age.

The assignment was to explain the proverb, "Tell me with whom you associate and I will tell you who you are." Gaston wrote:

This means, tell me what are the qualities and the faults of the children with whom you play and I will tell you what your qualities and faults are.

It expresses a truth of which we often see the proof. In school, one sees many friends, intelligent students choose intelligent friends, lazy students choose those who are like themselves. What makes these groups come together in the first place is common interests, and the pleasure derived from their association causes them to stay together.

I, for example, look for friends who are good and honest, and I will be their friend. If by accident I am mistaken and one of my friends turns out to be bad, I try to make him reform and if I don't succeed, I drop him.

Cyr's comments were: "A little short, which is too bad. There are some well-turned phrases and some ideas which are well expressed." In the margin he wrote many suggestions for improving the syntax. He gave his son a grade of 6½.

The triumph of middle-class values is apparent when comparing Cyr and Gaston Bigot. For Cyr, whose childhood was set in a rural world with school and its values superimposed on a traditional culture, there was a struggle between tradition and change.[10] Gaston never experienced this conflict; by the age of eleven, he was writing paragraphs that illustrated a school-formed mentality.

Acceptance of values taught in school books was also found in the notebooks of a girl from Bourges in 1914. It was of particular interest to study this girl's compositions because she was surely taught from *La Petite Jeanne* and other books by Carraud widely used in Bourges. The girl was asked to compose a piece about a clean student and one who was not so clean. She wrote:

It is 8:00 A.M., Jeanne enters her class, a pretty little girl! She is so clean that one takes pleasure just looking at her. Her face is well washed, her hair is combed nicely and tied back at the top of her head with a blue ribbon. Her outfit is simple, without too much decoration and with no stains. Her shoes are well shined and her hands are spotless. Her ears are very clean. It is time to start work. Jeanne sits down at her place and opens her school bag. What perfect order! What cleanliness! The books and notebooks are nicely covered, well ordered, no stains, no marks, everything is clean. How nice it is to see a pretty little girl. In our class, all the little girls take care of themselves well. There are some, however, who are sometimes not too clean; they may forget to clean their shoes or to brush them, but I don't know any who are really dirty.

While running errands, I met Marie, a little girl who was always absent from class. One hardly ever sees her going to school. And is she ever an example of a dirty child! Marie is not ugly, but she is always so messy that one can hardly see her pretty cheeks. Her hands are always black. Her dress is always poorly put together and is frequently torn in many places and dirty. A piece of her slip is always hanging out. She wears an old scarf which is tied around her head and is also very dirty. Nobody can tell what color it is. Oh, what a dirty little girl! If she comes into our class, I would not like to sit next to her. Dirtiness is something which I find shameful. That's why Marie stays far away from us. Let us always remember this proverb: Cleanliness is the wealth of the poor.

Mme. Imbault, the girl's teacher, commented: "Your style is correct and flows nicely. The two portraits are well-sketched. Avoid repetition and introducing so many phrases with who and that." It is clear from this composition, and several others, that this pupil thinks of herself as a good, clean little girl who will grow up to be a good mother. It is also clear that Zulma Carraud's *La Petite Jeanne* had become part of the consciousness of this little girl. She modeled the portraits of Jeanne and Marie in her composition after the characters of Jeanne and Marguerite in Carraud's book.

Finally, turning to the notebooks of Juliette Devilliers, born in 1880 in Catillon, a tiny village in the department of Oise, we return to the theme of the separation of the world of women from that of men. Devilliers began her studies in the communal school in 1884 and continued at a boarding school funded by the Sisters of Saint Joseph in Formière in 1890. In 1895 she wrote a composition on the reciprocal duties of brothers and sisters which demonstrated her acceptance of the ideas prevalent in the schoolbook literature of her day. Juliette stressed that brothers and sisters must always come to each other's aid. But how? "Brothers are more active, more expansive, and also more serious . . . Sisters aid their mothers in taking care of all the household duties."

The assumption that household duties and child care was somehow natural work for girls was expressed by Juliette as follows: "If the mother passes on, it is up to the oldest sister to replace her in as many ways as possible and to make the other children forget the pain of having lost their mother." If the father dies, it was, likewise, in the opinion of Juliette and her mentors, the "duty" of the oldest daughter to earn some money to aid the family. The brothers were occupied with being "serious and expansive," that is, preparing for work which would be personally and economically rewarding in the future.

The work of Devilliers, and the others referred to above, are but a sample of several hundred notebooks collected from the last century. Collectively, pupils' compositions show receptivity to middle-class ideas, with a few notable exceptions (e.g., "Le travail est la mère de tous vices"). There are three additional sources which are valuable in assessing the outcome of the persistent efforts of teachers, school book writers, and school inspectors to socialize rural children to modern gender roles: first, the records of awards distributed to students in primary schools; second, marriage acts which recorded data concerning occupations of brides and grooms; third, memoirs of teachers from rural backgrounds. None of these sources, including the notebooks, yield statistically valid data about socialization, but they do turn up the volume on the hushed voices of the children of yesteryear.

Girls and boys all over France were given awards for punctuality, assiduousness, cleanliness, orderliness, religious devotion, as well as for handwriting, reading, and arithmetic. It is difficult to know how they felt about these prizes, but we have some clues from unique records of students' speeches, kept by the Frères de la

Doctrine Chrétienne in working class neighborhoods of Lyon. Though we are listening to the words of workers' children, their testimony is a useful indication of the thoughts of their rural counterparts. In many cases, these children were only one generation removed from the village. Rural traditions were still part of their lives because many were sent out to rural wet-nurses and many were living with relatives who had recently emigrated from the countryside. In 1840 a prize-winning graduate thanked his teachers in words similar to those found in *Maurice*:

Because of your efforts . . . we have been introduced to the paths of virtue and honor . . . Aglow with the double flame of education and instruction, we now have a chance to dispel the ignorance which would otherwise be forever at our door. We can now participate, without fear or danger, in the true progress which distinguishes our era so eminently under the gentle influence of your protective guidance. Our childhood, calm and peaceful, was enriched by experience, formed by habit and by a love for work. We are prepared for a happy, joyous future.[11]

"A happy future based on love of work" was the ideal accepted by this young graduate of modest background. Was this really how he felt or was it simply a required bow to the ideas of his teachers? A study of the annual awards given to pupils in the same schools sheds more light on the pupils' acceptance of new ideas. In 1840, Vincent Chavier, who won first prize for good conduct in the parish of Saint Nizier for three years in a row, also won first prize in geography, second prize in spelling, first in assiduousness, third in application, first in history, second in arithmetic, third in handwriting, and no prize in drawing. Many other pupils had similar records and families frequently had more than one accomplished student in their midst.

It is intriguing to speculate, based on the list of awards winners, about the diffusion of middle-class ways in poor families. The Bonnard family, for example, won awards consistently from 1837 to 1843. While Benoit, the elder brother, received awards for "assiduousness," "application," and "recitation," the necessary groundwork for future accomplishments, his younger brother, Michel, won all of those plus handwriting, spelling, arithmetic, history, geography, and drawing. In the Perret family, Jean-Louis, the eldest, won two awards; Etienne, the next in line, received four awards; and Adolphe, the youngest and apparently a poor student, learned enough from his brothers' examples to win an award for "application." [12]

Another indication of the changing attitudes influenced by school attendance and school books is found in the marriage records of the second half of the nineteenth century. The marriage acts of the Croix-Rousse are very useful in this regard because they list the profession of brides and grooms, and often of both sets of parents too. The overwhelming impression gained from a study of these records is that men and women from rural areas were redefining their occupational roles in the nineteenth century. Partially, this was due to urbanization and industrialization, but the schools and books also played a role in changing the views of young people of what was an appropriate professional listing for men and women who were about to marry.

A study of the first two hundred and fifty marriages listed in the Croix-Rousse in each of the years 1856, 1866, 1876, 1886, allows some conclusions to be drawn. With each passing decade, more men and women could sign their names, which suggests that more and more had become literate and probably had attended primary school.

Simultaneously, there was a significant change in occupational, categories which reflected the ideas being taught in primary schools about appropriate gender roles for modern men and women. New occupations such as railroad worker, business employee, hired mason were listed for men only. While the number of categories listed for women workers remained fairly stable during the four decades (climbing slowly from 27 to 34), those for men, double to begin with, moved ahead rapidly (from 53 to 86). Women clustered in traditional jobs such as seamstresses or opted for the one new category open only to women *sans profession* (no occupation).[13]

The growth of job categories for men presaged a significant improvement in the earning potential of men workers while the introduction of *sans profession* as a category reserved for women, confirmed an attitudinal change. In the earlier records when a bride did not work there was simply no mention of any occupation. Gradually, the category *sans profession* seemed to become a matter of pride. In 1856, for example, there was only one woman out of the two hundred and fifty samples who did not list an occupation. But the term *sans profession* was not yet placed on the record. In 1866, seventeen women were recorded in this new category; in 1876, twenty-three, and in 1886 the number rose to thirty-three.[14]

A final source which provides a glimpse of the changing values of rural France are the memoirs of the teachers of the Belle Epoque, collected by Jacques Ozouf. For example, the young man from Deux-Sèvres who explained why he became a teacher simultaneously gave evidence of new values taking root in the countryside:

My father was a weaver and my mother and grandparents took care of the house and fields. I always considered the profession of instructor or teacher as being the most wonderful of professions. Certainly, my parents had an enormous influence on my choice of this profession: (1) Because my parents were uneducated (my grandparents were illiterate) they talked continuously to me about the benefits of education and they often cited the example of people who were capable and educated. My very real desire to learn was therefore greatly encouraged; (2) Like my parents, I thought the teaching profession was quite enviable because the salary was fairly stable and sufficient, while at home we never seemed to have enough to get by on; (3) When I thought about my father, pushing the treadle hour after hour in the corner of the stable, weaving linen, I supposed that the profession of teacher would be much less tiring (I have since changed my mind!); (4) I should add that it was during that period of struggle for republican, nonclerical ideals (which my father defended and believed in vehemently) that I came to respect the lay teacher and felt the desire to teach later in life. I truly considered all priests and church people to be intolerant, dangerous, hypocritical beings.[15]

The memoirs repeatedly refer to illiterate and impoverished parents and grandparents who wish their children's lives to be different from their own. Secure salaries and an easier life are the hopes of these parents for their children. If they must change some of their ways to enter the gates of the secure group, then they will change.

Thus, the values of cleanliness, punctuality, and planning were accepted, not because peasants were convinced, like Marguerite and Frisé in Carraud's books, that they were good values, but beause they became convinced that a better life was possible. For this same reason, the hope of a better life—less strenuous, more secure, rural boys and girls gradually adopted the roles of Maurice and Jeanne.

CHAPTER TEN

Conclusion

As a result of a complex web of changes, material and ideological, what emerged at the end of the nineteenth century was a phenomenon I describe as the *pas de quatre*. In this dance there are four partners: A bourgeois woman, a bourgeois man, a working woman, and a working man. All dance to the same tune: "Man should be the economic support of his wife and children, while women should become the emotional support for the family." But, to go on with the metaphor, the song is a cacaphony of different lyrics sung at the same time.

The bourgeois woman sang a verse written by Eugénie Niboyet: "The child of the people passes from crèche to day-care, to school, to workshop. The child of the lady passes from the arms of the nurse, to the hands of a maid, to those of a governess . . . the bourgeois class alone brings together family life. There, the mother is the first educator of her children." [1] The bourgeois man sang a verse dictated by Guizot, whose main theme was competition, independence, free trade, and whose answer to poverty was — *"Enrichissez-vous!"*

The working woman sang the words of Jeanne: "Just because they are poor, does that mean our children should be dirty?" While the working man sang the words of Maurice: "Don't worry my good Françoise, you will lack for nothing, I promise you; have confidence in me."

In the following stanza, each opening verse was developed, producing an even greater confusion. The bourgeois woman sang of women's moral superiority; the bourgeois man sang of the duty of women to help out their families in every way—even if that meant temporarily working outside of the home; the working woman sang to God to help her earn enough to put food on the table; the working man argued that women are not real workers.

This *pas de quartre* was the result of urbanization, industrialization, and the gradual adoption of appropriate gender roles, as prescribed by the middle class in books they wrote for boys and girls of rural families who were coaxed into aspiring to the better life. In material terms, the net result was that poor women worked in sex-segregated occupations, hired by middle-class men, at low wages. The psychological consequences were more complex. Women who worked outside the home felt guilty about not being good mothers; their husbands felt guilty about not being good breadwinners. Women who stayed home and saw themselves as morally superior to men, felt uneasy about their working sisters, whose morality and hungry children worried them in turn. Male employers who were too busy to be concerned with the moral issues of female employment kept their consciences in line with the thought that these conditions were only temporary. The profit they enjoyed went a long way to assuage their guilt.

The net result, in terms of the quality of life, was that an improved standard of living gradually reached most French men and women in varying degrees and at various tempos, depending on the region. By the end of the nineteenth century it was difficult to find women who regularly stood while their husbands dined, but the man was still nominally "king of his castle." The woman took over the moral rule of the family. She had the confirmation of the priest, the teacher, and the doctor, of her moral superiority. Eve became Mary, the perfect Mother.

Appendix A

School Books in Use In Public Primary Schools
(Survey Conducted in 1888-89)

Author	Title	Publisher	Number of departments which require it
Abria	Méthode de lecture	Garnier	14
Adam	Lectures militaires	Hachette	18
Aicard	Le livre des petits	Delagrave	4
Allain	Fables choisies de La Fontaine	Delalain	3
Anselme	Le village	André Guédon	4
Aulard	Lectures courantes, 3 vol.	Hachette	28
Auvert	Syllabaire	Delagrave	2
Bachelet	Les hommes illustres de France	Roussière	1
Bahie	Lecture élémentaire	Oberthur (à Rennes).	10
Barracaud	Un village au XII et au XIX siècle	Librairie d'éducation de la jeunesse	1
Barrau	La patrie	Hachette	40
Idem	Livre de morale pratique	Idem	32
Idem	Devoirs des enfants	Idem	11
Idem	Choix gradué de cinquante sortes d'écritures (lectures des manuscrits)	Idem	21
Barré	Lecture élémentaire	A Tours	5

Author	Title	Publisher	Number of departments which require it
Béhagnon	Nouvelle épellation (petites leçons 1 et 2 livres)	Belin	53
Idem	Lecture pour la nouvelle épellation	Idem	1
Belèze	Syllabaire et premières lectures	Delalain	6
Idem	Lecture courante	Idem	4
Idem	Exercises de mémoire et de style	Idem	4
Idem	Dictées et lectures	Idem	4
Benner	Livre de patrie	G. Maurice	39
Bérillon	La bonne ménagère, livré de lecture	Gallot, à Auxerre	4
Bert (Paul)	Lectures sur l'histoire naturelle	Hachette	38
Idem	Lectures et leçons de choses.	Picard et Kaan	29
Berthon	Méthode simultanée de lecture et d'écriture (1 livret)	Godchaux	1
Berthon	Méthode simultanée de lecture et d'écriture (2e livre)	Godchaux	1
Bidard	L'éducation par la poésie	Gédalge	19
Bigot	Lectures choisies de français moderne	Hachette	14
Bigot (Charles)	Le petit Français	Maurice (G.)	2
Bizos	Fénelon	Lecène et Oudin.	1
Blanchet	Biographies des hommes illustres	Belin	1
Bonnier	Leçons de choses	Paul Dupont	17
Bouant (E.)	Leçons de choses	Delalain	7
Boucher (Aug.)	Morceaux choisis de littérature française, 1ere partie	Belin	1
Idem	2e partie	Idem	1
Idem	3e partie	Idem	1
Bourcier	La prestolégie	Jonglard (à Gap)	2
Bourgoin	L'utile et l'agréable	Thouvenin	1
Bourguin	M. Lesage	Gauguet	7
Braud	Les premières leçons par coeur	Delagrave	9
Idem	Les secondes leçons par coeur	Idem	9

Author	Title	Publisher	Number of departments which require it
Bruno	Premier livre de lecture et d'instruction pour l'enfance.	Belin	66
Idem	Premier livre de lecture et d'instruction pour l'adolescent.	Idem	53
Idem	Livre de lecture pour adolescence	Idem	56
Idem	Le tour de France par deux enfants	Idem	73
Idem	Le Tour de France (partie du maître)	Idem	26
Idem	Francinet	Idem	66
Idem	Francinet (partie du maître).	Idem	23
Idem	Les enfants de Marcel	Idem	23
Idem	Les enfants de Marcel (partie du maître)	Idem	12
Buffon	Morceaux choisis	Idem	3
Bujon	Simples lectures sur l'histoire de Paris	Marpon	1
Calemard de la Fayette.	Petit Pierre ou le bon culti-vateur	Hachette	11
Caron	Lectures morales, historiques et scientifiques	Belin	5
Carraud (Mme.)	Maurice ou le travail	Hachette	23
Idem	Contes et historiettes	Idem	12
Idem	Petite Jeanne	Idem	21
Caumont	Les écoliers français	Delagrave	73
Idem	Récitation	Idem	33
Chabaud	Lectures des Français	Picard et Kaan	21
Chalamet	Première année d'économie domestique.	Colin	17
Charavay	L'héroisme civil	Librairie d'édu-cation de la jeunesse	1
Chasles (E.)	Livre de lecture	Delagrave	10
Chaumeil	Lectures alternées	Gédalge	47
Chéron	Tableaux de lecture	Delagrave	4
Idem	Livret de lecture	Idem	2
Idem	Premier livre de lecture	Idem	5

Author	Title	Publisher	Number of departments which require it
Chervin	Lecture à haute voix	Jeandé	9
Idem	Exercises de lecture	Idem	6
Idem	Résumé des principes et des exercises de lecture à haute voix	Idem	1
Chomel	Méthode de lecture	Fouraut	2
Christiaens et Arnold	Nouvelle méthode de lecture pour l'enseignement de l'écriture et de l'orthographe	Belin	36
Clayton	L'amour sacré de la patrie	Picard et Kaan	7
Collas	Mosaïque des écoles	Fouraut	18
Idem	Tableau de la France	Idem	2
Collin (Mme.)	Recueil de lectures choisies	Alcan	18
Colomb (Mme.)	Histoire de matou	Maurice (G.)	4
Compayré et Delplan	Lectures morales et civiques	Delaplane	49
Comte et Jeanvrot	La patrie française	Librairie d'éducation de la jeunesse	4
Conan	Trésor scientifique des écoles	Delagrave	10
Cons	Biographies d'hommes illustres	Idem	13
Corne	Maximes et proverbes	Hachette	6
Corréard	Michelet	Lecène et Oudin	13
Cortambert	Les trois règnes de la nature	Hachette	13
Couton	Lecture simplifiée	Delalain	6
Creutzer and Wirth	Nouvelles leçons de lecture courante	Delagrave	8
Cuir	Les petits écoliers	Hachette	53
Cuissart	Méthode de lecture et d'écriture (cinq tableaux)	Picard et Kaan	67
Idem	Premier degré de lectures courantes	Idem	51
Idem	Deuxieme degré de lectures courantes	Idem	54
Idem	Troisième degré de lectures courantes	Idem	40
Daniel	Choix de lectures	Hachette	10
Defodon	Choix de Fables	Idem	26

Author	Title	Publisher	Number of departments which require it
Delapalme	Livre de l'enfance et de l'adolescence	Idem	43
Idem	Le livre des petits enfants	Idem	24
Delapierre et la Marche (De)	Exercises de mémoire (cours élémentaire)	Picard et Kaan	38
Idem	Exercises de mémoire (cours moyen)	Idem	28
Idem	Exercises de mémoire (cours supérieur)	Idem	27
Idem	Exercises de poésie. Fables, poésies, maximes (cours élémentaire)	Idem	1
Idem	Exercises de poésie. Fables, poésies, maximes (cours moyen)	Idem	1
Idem	Idem. (Cours supérieur)	Idem	1
Delon	Les paysans	Librairie d'éducation de la jeunesse	11
Idem	Simples lectures	Hachette	9
Idem	Lectures expliquées	Idem	17
Idem	Notre capitale: Paris	Maurice (G.)	1
Delplan	La patrie et les patriotes	Paul Delaplane	52
Idem	La Révolution française	Idem	1
Deltour	Composition et style	Delagrave	3
Déroulède	Chants patriotiques français	Delagrave	24
Descubes	L'art et les artistes	Delaplane P.	7
Dhombres et Monod	Récits et biographies histori-ques (1ere partie, histoire ancienne)	Alcan F.	1
Idem	Récits et biographies histori-ques (2e partie, moyen âge et temps modernes.)	Idem	1
Ditandy	Cours pratique de lecture intelligente et expressive	Belin	10
Divers	Album littéraire de la France (XIV, XVII, XVIII et XIX S.)	Lecène et Oudin	1
Idem	Cours pratique de lecture partie du maître)	Idem	3

Author	Title	Publisher	Number of departments which require it
Douville	Syllabaire	Garnier	1
Dubois	Leçons de M. Henri	Gedalge	10
Idem	Gerbe de l'écolier (3 cours)	Idem	20
Idem	Récits Paternels	Idem	3
Ducros	Morceaux choisis	André Guédon	7
Idem	Jean-Jacques Rousseau	Lecène et Oudin	2
Duhamel	Livre de lecture des écoles primaires	Delagrave	2
Dunand	Méthode de lecture	Fouraut	9
Dupont	Grands tableaux citolégiques	Ducroq	37
Idem	Lectures graduées	Idem	29
Idem	Conversations enfantines	Idem	17
Idem	Premières connaissances usuelles	Idem	18
Idem	Citolégie	Idem	17
Dupuis (F.)	Premières Lectures	Delagrave	21
Idem	La France en Zigzag	Idem	40
Idem	Premières leçons de choses	Idem	29
Idem	Les vacances de l'instituteur (lectures manuscrites)	Idem	1
Dupuy (Ern.)	Victor Hugo	Lecène et Oudin	6
Durand	Lectures expliquées	Idem	5
Idem	Lectures choisies sur l'histoire de notre patrie	Hachette	19
Duruy (George)	Pour la France	Hachette	50
Duthar	Lectures choisies	Delagrave	2
Duval	Notre pays	Hachette	6
Etienne	Fablier des écoles	Fouraut	30
Etienne et Daniel	Premier livre de récitation et de morale	Vᵉ Larousse et Cie	5
Idem	Second Livre de récitation et de morale	Idem	30
Fabre	Le Ciel	Delagrave	10
Idem	La terre	Idem	15
Idem	Les petites filles	Idem	35
Idem	Aurore	Idem	43
Idem	Le Ménage	Idem	60
Idem	Les Libérateurs	Idem	31

Author	Title	Publisher	Number of departments which require it
Idem	Jeanne d'Arc	Idem	11
Idem	Le livre des champs	Idem	25
Idem	Auxiliaires et ravageurs (2 vol.)	Idem	30
Idem	Leçons de choses	Idem	7
Idem	Le livre d'histoire, récits scientifiques de l'oncle Paul à ses neveux	Idem	61
Idem	L'industrie	Idem	8
Idem	Lecture, 2e et 3^{e}années (maîtres et élèves)	Idem	3
Faguet	La Fontaine	Lecène et Oudin	7
Idem	Corneille	Idem	4
Fénelon	Morceaux choisis avec notes de Caroc	Belin	3
Idem	Fables	Idem	9
Feugère	Morceaux choisis	Delalain	11
F.I.C.	Livre-tableau	Mame et Pousielgue	9
Idem	Lectures courantes	Idem	7
Figurier	Les grandes inventions	Hachette	27
Fleuriot	Première année de récitation	Jeandé	5
Florian	Fables	Delalain	21
Idem	Idem	Belin	3
Idem	Idem	Hachette	5
Fourcade	Nouvelle méthode simultanée de lecture, d'écriture et d'orthographe, à l'usage des des écoles maternelles et primaires.	Chez l'auteur (à St. Maur (Gers)	5
Frémont	Fables de Fénelon	Delalain	2
Frétille	Secondes leçons de lecture	Delagrave	2
F.T. et J.	Méthode de lecture	Lamarzelle (à Vannes)	3
Garrigues	Simples lectures sur les sciences	Hachette	39
Garsault	Causeries d'un grand-père	Idem	9
Gauguet	Premier livre de lecture	Thouvenin	1

Author	Title	Publisher	Number of departments which require it
Idem	Deuxième livre de lecture	Idem	1
Idem	Nouveau choix de fables françaises	Idem	1
Gaultié	Cours méthodique de lecture	Gauguet	5
Gellion-Danglar	La nationalité et la langue françaises	Degorce-Cadot	3
Georges et Troncet	Lectures intuitives	Ve Larousse et Cie.	47
Idem	Lectures intuitives (1ere livre)	Idem	11
Idem	Lectures intuitives (2^{e}années	Idem	11
Georgin	Premières leçons de lecture	Paul Dupont	15
Gérardin	Les Plantes	Masson	11
Idem	Les Bêtes	Idem	11
Idem	La Terre	Idem	11
Germain et Aubert	La Révolution:ses bienfaits	Allison	1
Gérusez	Fables de La Fontaine	Hachette	14
Gidel	Livre d'enfant	Delagrave	11
Gillet Damitte	Livre de récitation	Delalain	1
Gleyre (Mlle.) et PapeCarpantier (Mme.)	Choix de récitations expliquées	Boulanger	7
Goepp et Ducoudray	Le Patriotisme en France	Hachette	14
Gossin	Lectures choisies	Gautier	9
G.R.	Les lectures du soldat	Delagrave	1
Gresse	Premières lectures courantes	Picard et Kaan	6
Idem	Méthode de lecture	Idem	6
Grimbert	Petite encyclopédie des écoles (1ere et 2e semestre)	Garnier	1
Grimblot	Le savoir et le devoir de l'enfance	Ve Larousse et Cie.	6
Grisot	Morceaux choisis de littérature française	Belin	5
Grosselin	Méthode phonomimique	Pigoreau	39
Idem	Exercises gradués de lectures courantes	Idem	7
Idem	Alphabet phonétique	Idem	1

Author	Title	Publisher	Number of departments which require it
Grosselin	Enseignement phonomimique de la lecture (grands gestes)	Pigoreau	1
Idem	Enseignement phonomimique de la lecture (26 tableaux)	Idem	1
Guérin	Premières lectures	Hachette	18
Idem	Lectures et grammaire	Idem	6
Gugenberger	Enseignement simultané de la lecture et des manuscrits	Ve Larousse et Cie.	15
Guillemot	La semaine de l'enfant	Delagrave	3
Guy	Les femmes françaises	G. Maurice	1
Guyau	Lectures courantes:année enfantine	Colin	76
Idem	Lectures courantes:année préparatoire	Idem	76
Hanriot	Vive la France	Picard et Kaan	67
Idem	Choix de lectures pour l'année	Delagrave	17
Heinrich	Lectures choisies	Fouraut	13
Hément	Menus propos sur les sciences	Delagrave	9
Henrion	Méthode de lecture avec l'ancienne épellation	Belin	39
Idem	Le monde des jeunes filles	Idem	12
Idem	La science des enfants	Idem	31
Idem	Le monde des adolescents	Idem	31
Idem	Les champs et les jardins	Idem	8
Henry	Lectures morales, historiques et scientifiques	Idem	4
Henry (Gervais)	Syllabateur avec cartons	Hachette	3
Idem	Tableau de lecture	Idem	3
Idem	Livret de lecture	Idem	3
Herbault	Cours complet de littérature: éléments de style	Ducrocq	4
Idem	Cours complet de litt: morceaux choisis de littérature (prose et vers)	Idem	4
Huë (Sophie)	Les Maternelles	Phihon et Hervé (à Rennes)	4
Humbert	L'art de bien lire	Ve Larousse et Cie.	15
Idem	Le fablier de la jeunesse	Garnier	16

Author	Title	Publisher	Number of departments which require it
Instituteur (un)	Choix gradué de 50 Fables	Delagrave	7
Idem	Petite école de lecture	Renaud (à Dijon)	4
Instituteurs (Plusiers)	Méthode de lecture	Delagrave	7
Jannetaz	Morceaux choisis d'auteurs classiques	Paul Dupont	17
Jeannel	Petit Jean	Delagrave	20
Jost, Broeunig et Humbert	Lectures pratiques	Hachette	80
Idem.	Histoires et causeries morales	Delagrave	5
Julian	Orthophonic	Beaumevielle (à Montpellier)	4
Juranville (Mlle.)	Le savoir-vivre et le savoir-faire	Ve Larousse et Cie.	49
Idem	Le premier livre des petites filles	Idem	49
Idem	Le deuxième livre des petites filles	Idem	24
Idem	Lectures intermèdiaires	Idem	7
Jussieu (De)	Simon de Nantua	Librairie d'éducation de la jeunesse	7
Kergomard (Mme.)	Les biens de la terre	Fischbacher	78
Idem	Un sauvetage	Idem	53
L'Abbé	Morceaux choisis des classiques français	Hachette	29
Lachambaudie	Choix de Fables	Delagrave	1
La Fontaine	Fables (Ed. Colincamp)	Delagrave	37
Idem	Fables (A. Gazier)	Colin	17
Idem	Fables annotés par Buffon	Johaust	7
Idem	Fables (ed. Aubertin)	Belin	5
Idem	Fables choisies (notes de Caron)	Idem	5
Idem	Cent Fables choisies (notes de Caron	Idem	8
Idem	Fables (éd. Defodon)	Hachette	9
Idem	Les Fables (édition Rouzé)	Belin	1

Author	Title	Publisher	Number of departments which require it
Lalanne	Les poésies de l'enfance	Belin	1
Langlois-Fréville	Traité de lecture et de pronunciation	Tresse	1
Lanier	Lecture géographiques: L'Europe	Belin	3
Idem	Lecture géographiques: L'Afrique	Idem	3
Idem	Lectures géographiques: L'Amérique	Idem	3
Larousse	Méthode lexicologique de	Ve Larousse et Cie.	38
Larousse et Boyer	Trésor poétique	Idem	5
Lavallette	Les enfants modèles	Picard et Kaan	57
Idem	Premières connaissances de l'âge d'or	Idem	57
Idem	Secondes connaissances	Idem	38
Idem	Nouvelle méthode de lecture	Idem	7
Idem	La lecture enseignée	Idem	4
Lavigne et X	Le Voltaire des écoles	Delagrave	1
Lavinay	Choix de lectures des enfants	Idem	7
Lavisse (Emile)	Tu seras soldat	Colin	26
Lebaigue	Morceaux choisis de littérature française (1ere année)	Belin	23
Idem	(2e année)	Idem	12
Idem	Le livre de l'école. Choix de lecture expliquée (classe enfantine)	Idem	64
Idem	(Classe préparatoire)	Idem	33
Idem	Le livre de l'école (choix de lecture expliquée) Classe élémentaire	Belin	37
Idem	(Cours moyen)	Idem	(37)
Idem	(Cours supérieur)	Idem	34
Lebaigue et Pessonneaux	Lectures expliquées. Recueil de morceaux choisis	Idem	16
Lebasteur	Buffon	Lecène et Oudin	1
Lebrun	Livre de lecture courante	Hachette	35

Author	Title	Publisher	Number of departments which require it
Le Coz	Méthode de lecture	Guyon (à Saint Brieuc)	11
Lefrançais	Lectures patriotiques	Delagrave	38
Legouvé	L'art de la lecture	Hetzel	10
Idem	Petit traité de lecture	Idem	1
Leguidre	Industrie manufacturière	Delagrave	16
Le Mercier	Méthode de lecture	Anger (à Pontivy)	1
Lemonnier	L'Algérie	Librairie d'édu-cation de jeunesse	3
Leroy (Ch.)	Lectures graduées et leçons pratiques de litt. et de style (prose et poésie)	Belin	3
Leroy (Ch)	Flore poétique du jeune âge	Belin	1
Leroy (Th)	L'anthologie française des écoles primaires	Idem	10
Idem	La vie champêtre (série de lectures manuscrits)	Idem	21
Lesesue	Méthode de lecture intuitive	Fouraut	1
Liard	Lectures morales et littéraires	Belin	41
Linden	Historiettes du grand-papa Gilbert	Delagrave	9
Lorrain	Récits patriotiques	Hachette	57
Loye	Méthode de lecture	Mulcey (à Cha-lons-sur-Saône)	2
Lutz (Mme.)	Lecture pour les enfants des classes élémentaires	J. Lévy	1
Maigne	Lectures variées sur les sciences usuelles	Belin	39
Idem	Histoire de l'industrie	Idem	16
Idem	Nouvelles leçons de choses sur l'industrie, le commerce et les principales inventions industrielles.	Idem	19
Idem	Petites leçons sur les prin-cipales inventions industrielles et les principales industries	Idem	10
Idem	Nouvelles leçons de choses	Belin	21

Author	Title	Publisher	Number of departments which require it
	sur l'industrie et le commerce (partie du maître)		
Mainard	A travers la vie	Lib. d'éducation de la jeunesse	9
Idem	La vie enfantine	Idem	8
Maître	Tableaux de lecture	Hachette	5
Manuel	Poésies du foyer et de l'école	Calmann Lévy	4
Manuel et Alvarès	Abrégé de la France	Delagrave	35
Idem	La France (4 vol.)	Idem	30
Marcou	Les lectures du premier âge	Garnier	8
Idem	Les lectures de l'école (en 3 parties)	Idem	16
Marguerin	Recueil de morceaux choisis (3 vol.)	Delagrave	9
Martin	Leçons graduées de lectures manuscrites	Delagrave	1
Masson	Livre de lecture des petits garçons	Hachette	12
Matrat (Marie)	Lectures enfantines	Dupont (P.)	10
Idem	L'Education maternelle	Idem	12
Mayer	Chez nous	Delagrave	5
Méchin	Fleurs et épines ou vertus et défauts	Belin	2
Merlet	Extrait des classiques français	Fourant	15
Messin	Lectures quotidiennes	Gédalge	9
Idem	Récits enfantins	Ducrocq	20
Messin et Lebéalle	Lectures manuscrites sur le dessin	Gédalge	10
Michel	Méthode de lecture	Delagrave	49
Michelet	Les grandes journées de la Révolution	Hetzel	2
Mir	Enseignement de la lecture par l'écriture (3 livrets)	Pigoreau	9
Monget et Guérin	Introduction à la lecture	Dupont (P.)	7
Monternault (Mme.)	Les Saisons	Hachette	6
Mory	Nouvelle méthode de lecture et d'écriture par l'aspect	Librairie Nouvelle	1

Author	Title	Publisher	Number of departments which require it
Mottot	Méthode de lecture d'après les nouveaux procédés mnémo-techniques (syllabaire, premier livret, deuxième livret)	Belin	18
Mougeol	Contes, paraboles, anecdotes	Delagrave	2
Idem	Historiettes morales	Idem	1
Naudet	Poésies de la jeunesse	Paul Dupont	11
Néel	Méthode de lecture (3 livres et 2 tableaux)	Colin	65
Niaudet	Un peu de tout ce qu'il est bon de savoir	Gédalge	5
Noël	Tableaux de lecture	Idem	40
Idem	Syllabaire	Idem	29
Idem	Nouvelle lecture rationnelle	Idem	45
Noël et Fleury	Cent leçons de récitation	Belin	21
Idem	Soixante-dix leçons de récitations	Idem	15
Nonus	Lecture courante	Boyer (Paul) [à Châlons-sur-Saône]	11
Pape-Carpantier (Mme.)	Syllabaire	Hachette	16
Idem	Premières lectures	Idem	19
Idem	Histoire du blé	Idem	15
Idem	Lectures et travail	Idem	13
Parent	Premières lectures courantes	Idem	13
Pascal	Le livre de l'élève soldat	Idem	14
Pécaut	Petit livre de lecture	Idem	33
Pécaut et Baude	L'art, simples entretiens	Ve Larousse et Cie.	9
Peigné	Tableaux de lecture	Fouraut	14
Idem	Méthode de lecture	Belin	14
Pélissier	Gymnastique de l'esprit	Hachette	29
Pelletan	La Naissance d'une ville	Alcan	7
Peloni	Méthode d'enseignement simultanée de la lecture etc. (1 livret, 5 tableaux)	Bricon	1
Petit	Lectures tirées d' auteurs modernes	Picard et Kaan	1

Author	Title	Publisher	Number of departments which require it
Pichard	120 Lectures	Pigoreau	3
Idem	Lectures enfantines	Idem	15
Idem	Récitations du samedi	Idem	19
Pichard (Lilla)	La bonne petite fille	Belin	1
Idem	Mme. Adeline, récits d'une institutrice sur l'intelligence des animaux	Idem	1
Pinard	Civilité	Fouraut	2
Pinet (Mme.)	Récréations de l'école	Delalain	2
Pinet et Naudet	Lectures manuscrites sur l'agriculture	Dupont (P.)	3
Plateau et Caumont	Lectures courantes (Haute-Marne)	Delagrave	6
Ploërmel (Frères de)	Nouvelle méthode simultanée de lecture, d'écriture et d' orthographie, à l'usage des écoles maternelles et primaires	à Ploërmel	2
Poiré	Simples lectures sur les principales industrielles	Hachette	15
Idem	Premières notions sur l'industrie	Idem	19
Porchat	Fablier des écoles	Delagrave	15
Idem	Trois mois sous la neige	Idem	5
Idem	Les colons du rivage	Idem	3
Pourret	Lectures familières sur le travail industriel	Fouraut	8
Pressard	Lectures morales et littéraires	Hachette	17
Ratisbonne	Comédie enfantine (2 vol.)	Delagrave	16
Regimbeau	Méthode de lecture (syllabaire)	Hachette	61
Idem	Petit syllabaire	Idem	9
Idem	Premiers exercises d'écriture et d'orthographe	Idem	8
Idem	Tableau mural pour l'enseignement de la lecture	Idem	1

Author	Title	Publisher	Number of departments which require it
Idem	Syllabaire-Atlas ou livre tableau pour l'enseignement de la lecture	Idem	1
Renard	Les étapes d'un petit Algérien	Idem	2
Renard et Martine	Zigszags à travers les choses usuelles	Nathan	34
Rendu	Récits moraux et instructifs	Fouraut	6
Idem	Lectures des manuscrits	Idem	7
Idem	Les Français	Idem	8
Reusse et Scalbert	Le petit Paul	Delagrave	1
Richard	Syllabaire	Wilmot (à Lille)	10
Ricquier	Recueil de morceaux choisis (4 vol.)	Delagrave	14
Idem	Méthode de lecture à haute voix	Belin	8
Idem	Méthode de lecture à haute voix et de récitation	Delagrave	1
Idem	Poésies, récits	Idem	1
Idem	Lectures et récitations pour les enfants de 6 à 10 ans	Idem	1
Riom	Choix de Fables	Larousse	9
Idem	Méthode de lecture	Vernay	1
Roche	Les martyrs du travail	Delagrave	4
Rocherolles	Premières lectures enfantines	Colin	77
Idem	Secondes lectures enfantines	Idem	74
Idem	Troisième lectures enfantines	Idem	70
Rousselot	Leçons de choses	Delagrave	19
Idem	Exercises de récitation	Idem	16
Roux et Hanriot	Exercises de récitation	Colin	9
Saffray (Dr.)	Leçons de choses	Hachette	40
Idem	Eléments des sciences physiques et naturelles (cours élémentaire)	Idem	1
Idem	Eléments des sciences physiques et nat. (cours moyen)	Idem	1
Saint-Surin	Paul Morin	Fouraut	2
Sarradon	Méthode de lecture	Delagrave	9
Sauvageot et	Cours simultané de lecture	Delagrave	19

Author	Title	Publisher	Number of departments which require it
Séguin			
Idem	Orthographe	Idem	1
Schmid	100 nouveaux petits contes	Hachette	9
Schuler	Enseignement simultané de la lecture et de l'écriture	Idem	15
Soc. d'inspecteurs	Choix de méthodes de lecture	Belin	14
Soulice	Premières connaissances	Hachette	9
Idem	Lectures manuscrites	Fouraut	4
Souvestre	Lectures journalières	Calmann Lévy	2
Idem	Un philosophe sous les toits	Idem	1
Idem	Au coin du feu	Idem	1
Subercaze	Premier livre de récitation	Delalain	9
Idem	Premier livre de lectures	Idem	4
Tarrène	Règles de la lecture à haute voix	Hachette	2
Taulier	André ou la ferme de Meylan	Belin	3
Théodore	Méthode naturelle pour apprendre à la fois la lecture et l'écriture	Delagrave	3
Thèze	Lectures graduées	Fouraut	4
Tolstoi	Pour les enfants	Savine	1
Tournemire	La mére institutrice ou l'éducateur	Idem	—
Toussaint	Méthode de lecture (1 livre et 12 tableaux)	Delagrave	3
Idem	Petit livre de lectures graduées	Idem	1
Turgan	150 lectures littéraires	Bacon	1
Idem	100 lectures littéraires	Idem	1
Valade-Gabel	Des faits à l'idée	Delagrave	3
Valette (Mme.)	La journée de la petite ménagère	Maurice (G.)	22
Idem	La petite ménagère	Idem	6
Vessiot	La récitation à l'école et la lecture expliquée	Lecène et Oudin	9
Idem	Pour nos enfants	Idem	10
Viaud	Manuscrit scolaire	Colin	15
Viaud et Langmier	Morceaux choisis et récitation	Baltenweck	1

Author	Title	Publisher	Number of departments which require it
Vicaire et Leser	Le livre de la Patrie	Maurice (G.)	1
Vieuville	La France nouvelle, essai de réforme morale pour enfants	Ve Larousse et Cie.	3
Villemereux	Méthode de lecture	Paul Dupont	30
Vincent	Nos fabulistes	Barbou, à Limoges	9
Idem	Histoire de la France et du peuple français	Gédalge	1
Vincent et Magé	Lectures et récitations expliquées	Delaplane (P.)	34
Vincent P. et Vincent (Mlle.)	Lectures et récitations expliquées (cours élémentaire)	Idem	1
Vinson (J.)	Choix de lectures en vers	Librairie d'éducation laïque	1
Vinson (J.)	Choix de lectures en prose	Idem	1
Vinsot et Renaudin	Lectures manuscrites	Ve Larousse et Cie.	9
Wilm	Premières lectures françaises	Berger-Levrault	8
Wirth. (Mlle.)	Le livre de lecture courante	Hachette	21
Idem	La future ménagère	Idem	15
Wirth (Mlle.) et Bret (Mlle.)	Premières leçons d'économie domestique	Idem	29
X	Livres de lectures choisies en prose et en vers (1ere part.)	Lemerre	1
Zidler	Une lecture par semaine	Paul Dupont	3
Idem	Mosaïque des écoles	Idem	2
	Album littéraire de la France	Lecéne et Oudin	1
	Lectures du soldat	Delagrave	1

Appendix B

The following charts permit a comparison between a rich region—the Rhône—and a poor one—the Corréze. Inspector's reports from 1835-1836 from the two areas were juxtaposed to permit a view of the uneven response to the Guizot laws, with regard to teachers, pupils, and students.

Table1. Representative figures for the comparison between communal and private schools

Department	Number of communities or larger subdivisions in the region	Number of communities or larger subdivisions					Population in the communities or larger subdivision
		that have schools	that have no school	that can afford only one school either for boys or girls because of the poverty of the population	that have a private school for boys or girls, but do not have a communal school for boys yet	that could have a special school for girls, but do not have one	
Lyon	129	120	5	24	7	5	330,004
Villefranche	118	107	11	17	3	7	151,980
Total for the Rhône	243	227	16	41	10	12	482,024
Tulle	118	53	65	79	2	39	129,799
Brive	101	50	51	76	1	25	113,094
Ussel	74	18	56	60	—	14	59,540
Total for the Corrèze	293	121	172	215	3	78	302,433

Table 2. Number of communal and private primary schools for boys and for girls

Department	Number of communal primary schools for boys		Number of communal primary boys' schools		Number of communal primary schools specially reserved for girls	Number of private primary schools				General total for schools
	that should be supported by the communities of the region	that are actually supported by them	specially reserved for boys	mixed schools		for boys	for girls	mixed schools	Total	
Lyon	148	148	129	19	124	70	52	15	137	419
Villefranche	120	120	99	21	88	20	22	5	47	255
Total for the Rhône	268	268	228	40	212	90	74	20	184	674
Tulle	119	54	47	7	2	9	17	—	26	82
Brive	102	51	51	—	3	7	13	—	20	74
Ussel	74	18	16	2	2	4	9	—	13	33
Total for the Corrèze	295	123	114	9	7	20	39	—	59	189

Table 3. Personal situation of boys' and girls' teachers

Department	Number of communal boys' teachers and assistants		Number of communal girls' teachers and assistants		Number of private boys' teachers and assistants		Number of private girls' teachers and assistants		Number of secular boys' teachers and assistants			Number of secular girls' teachers and assistants		
	secular	*who belongs to a religious congregation*	*secular*	*who belongs to a religious congregation*	*secular*	*who belongs to a religious congregation*	*secular*	*who belongs to a religious congregation*	*married*	*widowers*	*bachelors*	*married*	*widows*	*unmarried*
Lyon	122	66	24	100	75	0	62	0	62	3	132	20	5	61
Villefranche	119	15	32	56	22	0	25	0	67	2	68	14	4	39
Total for the Rhône	237	81	56	196	97	0	87	0	129	5	200	34	9	100
Tulle	53	4	1	2	9	—	18	8	23	4	35	6	—	13
Brive	50	4	3	—	7	—	13	—	32	5	20	4	1	11
Ussel	18	—	—	15	4	—	9	4	15	1	6	1	—	8
Total for Corrèze	121	8	4	17	20	—	40	12	70	10	61	11	1	32

Table 4. Teaching methods used in communal and private schools

Department	Number of communal primary schools for that use the following methods				Number of communal primary schools that use the following methods				Number of private primary schools directed by a man where the following methods are used				Number of private primary schools directed by a woman where the following methods are used			
	mutual	*simultaneous*	*individual*	*mixed*	*mutual*	*simultaneous*	*individual*	*mixed*	*mutual*	*simultaneous*	*individual*	*mixed*	*mutual*	*simultaneous*	*Individual*	*mixed*
Lyon	16	116	10	6	4	70	54	0	6	30	39	0	0	40	22	0
Villefranche	6	92	18	4	0	30	58	0	0	12	10	0	0	7	18	10
Total for the Rhône	22	208	28	10	4	100	112	0	6	42	49	0	0	47	18	0
Tulle	—	11	—	43	—	—	—	2	—	1	—	8	—	—	—	17
Brive	—	19	—	38	—	—	—	3	—	—	—	7	—	—	3	10
Ussel	—	5	—	13	—	—	—	2	—	—	1	3	—	—	1	8
Total for the Corrèze	—	29	—	94	—	—	—	7	—	1	1	18	—	—	4	35

Table 5. Number of children attending communal and private primary schools
(average number of students calculated on the data for the two academic years: 1835-36, 1836-1837)

| Department | Communal schools for boys | | Communal schools where both boys and girls are accepted | | | | Communal schools for girls | | Private schools directed by a man | | | | Private schools directed by a woman | | | | General totals for the number of children in communal and private primary schools | | | |
| | | | boys | | girls | | | | boys | | girls | | boys | | girls | | boys | | girls | |
	in winter	in summer	in winter	in summer	in winter	in summer	in winter	in summer	in winter	in summer	in winter	in summer	in winter	in summer	in winter	in summer	in winter	in summer	in winter	in summer
Lyon	10,002	7,200	460	115	400	140	8,479	5,150	2,200	1,800	108	40	90	60	1,860	1,500	12,752	9,175	10,847	6,837
Villefranche	6,729	3,842	400	105	450	225	5,361	3,592	600	200	90	64	64	15	1,180	600	7,793	4,162	7,081	4,471
Total for the Rhône	16,731	11,042	860	220	850	365	13,840	8,742	2,800	2,000	198	104	154	75	3,040	2,100	20,545	13,337	17,928	11,308
Tulle	1,931	1,307	214	113	34	28	190	172	268	262	—	—	—	—	649	567	2,413	1,569	873	766
Brive	2,098	1,422	—	—	—	—	84	84	143	113	—	—	—	—	816	761	2,241	1,535	900	845
Ussel	558	313	74	20	20	6	140	140	136	69	—	—	—	—	405	367	768	382	565	513
Total for the Corrèze	4,587	3,042	288	133	54	34	414	396	547	444	—	—	—	—	1,870	1,694	5,422	3,486	2,338	2,124

Table 6. Number of schools and their students, according to religion

| Department | Number of communal schools for boys | | | | Number of students who attended communal and private schools for boys and girls and who observe | | | | | |
| | Catholic | Protestant | Jewish | mixed | Catholicism | | Protestantism | | Judaism | |
					boys	girls	boys	girls	boys	girls
Lyon	137	1	0	10	12,590	10,701	154	140	8	6
Villefranche	120	0	0	0	7,793	7,081	0	0	0	0
Total for the Rhône	257	1	0	10	20,383	17,782	154	140	8	6
Tulle	54	—	—	—	2,413	—	—	—	—	—
Brive	51	—	—	—	2,241	—	—	—	—	—
Ussel	18	—	—	—	768	—	—	—	—	—
Total for Corrèze	123	—	—	—	5,422	2,338	—	—	—	—

Table 7. Number of poor who are getting education free of charge and for the teachers' income

| Department | Number of students who are getting primary education in communal schools | | Number of students | | | | Average amount of monthly contribution per student | | Approximate income of communal boys' teachers (average) | | Approximate income of communal girls' teachers (average) | |
| | | | who pay monthly contribution | | exempt from monthly contribution | | | | | | | |
	boys	girsl	boys	girls	boys	girls	for boys' and mixed schools	for girls' schools	fixed salary	monthly retribution	fixed	monthly retribution
Lyon	10,462	8,879	4,814	4,356	5,648	4,523	1,50	1,70	200	360	0	340
Villefranche	7,129	5,811	3,455	4,408	3,674	1,403	1,50	1,60	200	380	0	340
Total for the Rhône	17,591	14,690	8,269	8,764	9,322	5,926	1,50	1,65	200	370	0	340
Tulle	2,145	224	1,075	55	1,070	159	1,22	1,25	200	250	200	100
Brive	2,098	84	1,400	71	698	13	1,48	1,25	200	345	200	300
Ussel	632	140	474	40	158	100	1,28	3,50	200	360	500	1500
Total for	4,875	468	2,949	176	1,926	1,292	1,32	2,00	200	318	300	633

Table. 8. Classification of schools according to their effectiveness

Department	Number of communal schools for boys			Number of communal schools for girls			Number of private schools for boys			Number of private schools for girls		
	good discipline and teaching	mediocre	poorly directed	good discipline and teaching	mediocre	poorly directed	good discipline and teaching	mediocre	poorly directed	good discipline and teaching	mediocre	poorly directed
Lyon	96	42	10	46	56	22	20	42	23	12	26	14
Villefranche	68	38	14	28	41	19	6	7	12	5	9	8
Total for the Rhône	164	80	24	74	97	41	26	49	35	17	35	22
Tulle	good 10 · 23 · passing 13	24	7				3	5	1			
Brive	good 16 · 22 · passing 6	24	5				1	4	2			
Ussel	good 7 · 8 · passing 1	5	5				0	3	1			
Total for the Corrèze	good 33 · 53 · passing 20	53	17	5	3	0	4	12	4	16	19	4

182

Table 9. School buildings that are communal property

Department	Number of communities and larger subdivisions	How many among them possess school buildings		Total number of school buildings owned by communities	Number of buildings that are properly accommodated			Number of school buildings where both boys and girls meet in the same classroom	With partition in the middle of the class in order to separate boys from girls	Number of school buildings that need repairs or expansion	Total of expenses for that purpose	For how many buildings the municipal councils are ready to pay on the spot
		in sufficient number	*in insufficient number*		*spacious enough*	*for a school*	*and for teacher's lodging*					
Lyon	125	60	0	60	50	45	40	4	3	18	20,615	10
Villefranche	118	25	0	25	20	18	17	3	0	9	10,245	6
Total for the Rhône	243	85	0	85	70	63	57	7	3	27	30,860	16
Tulle	118	6	—	7	5	7	5	5	2	4	5,500	—
Brive	101	7	—	8	7	8	7	—	—	7	12,000	—
Ussel	74	2	—	2	—	2	—	6	4	2	7,000	—
Total for the Corrèze	293	15	—	17	12	17	12	1	6	13	24,500	—

Table 10. Representative statistics for the communities that do not possess school buildings

Department	Number of communities or larger subdivisions		Approximate evaluation of the necessary expenses to procure in these communities a properly accommodated school building	Number of those who announced their intention to vote funds to that expense immediately	Total of expenses due to the communities	Total of the amounts they offer to invest
	that have no school buildings	*that have buildings for some of their schools*				
Lyon	65	0	268,544	15	63,242	41,100
Villefranche	93	0	372,324	19	80,326	55,894
Total for the Rhône	158	0	640,868	34	143,568	96,994
Tulle	112	—	336,000	15	59,000	26,100 (voted 9,600)
Brive	94	—	282,000	14	44,000	27,000 (voted 11,772)
Ussel	72	—	216,000	7	25,000	7,700
Total for Corrèze	278	—	834,000	36	128,000	60,800

Table 11. Representative statistics for the classroom furniture in communal schools for boys and for girls

Department	Number of schools	Number of those whose furniture is the property of the community	Number of those whose furniture is insufficient	Total of expenses required for the purchase of necessary furniture when it is not in the communal possession, or for its completion when it is insufficient	Number of schools that possess sufficient furniture from the communal belongings	Number of those that have no communal furniture and whose furniture is insufficient and for which the municipal councils pay or will pay the expenses
Lyon	272	104	25	38,600	79	11
Villefranche	208	92	39	31,000	53	14
Total for the Rhône	480	196	64	69,600	132	25
Tulle	56	29	23	7,000	6	2
Brive	54	29	17	6,500	12	–
Ussel	20	5	4	3,600	1	–
Total for Corrèze	130	63	44	17,000	19	2

Notes

Introduction

1. Archives Municipale de Lyon, R¹, Projet de loi sur l'instruction primaire, January 1833, p.3.

2. Teachers who wrote children's books include: L. Bader, T. H. Barrau, Mme. Campan, Z. Carraud, Mme. Pape-Carpentier, Mlle. Sauvan. Clergy who wrote children's books: Frère Bernardin, L'Abbé Berrangen, L'Abbé Chevojon, L'Abbé Duval, L'Abbé Herbert-Duperron, L'Abbé Méchin. See Appendix A for complete list.

3. Theodore Zeldin, *France 1748-1945*, vol. 2 (Oxford: 1977), p. 141.

4. Adeline Daumard, "The Parisian Bourgeoise," in Peter Stearns, ed., *A Century for Debate* (New York: 1973), p. 149.

5. Cf. Sherri Ortner, "Male Is to Female As Culture Is to Nature," in Rosaldo and Lamphere, ed., *Women, Culture and Society*, Stanford: 1974.

6. Cf. Michel Melot, "La Mauvaise Mère, Etude d'un thème romantique dans l'estampe et la littérature," *Gazette des Beaux-Arts*, 1973, p. 167-176.

7. Cf. Pierrette Pezerot, "Petites Filles, petites femmes, ou la vertu nécessaire," *Les Temps Modernes*, May 1976, pp. 190-191. Pezerot asks how these women could advise limiting women's sphere. Her conclusion is that they didn't feel themselves to be victims. In her view, they completely internalized the masculine values of the triumphant bourgeoisie.

One: The Poverty of Rural Schools

1. P. Chevallier and B. Grosperrin, *L'Enseignement français de la Révolution à nos jours*, vol. II: Documents (Paris: Mouton, 1971), Rapport Condorcet, p. 11. *Projet de loi sur l'instruction primaire*, janvier 1833, p. 3.

3. André Magnoux, "L'enfance dans nos campagnes limousines d'autrefois," *Lemouzi*, no. 67, 1978, p. 176.

3. Ida Boyer, ed., *Lettres des Institutrices rurales d'autrefois*, (Paris, n.d.), p. 191.

4. Ibid.

5. A. Bouillon, *De la construction des maisons d'école primaire: ouvrage contenant des projets descriptifs et estimatifs pour six maisons d'école* (Paris: 1934).

6. Oral interview with M. Jean Pouch, Le Devès, Corrèze, Dec. 1976.

7. Sebillot, *Coutumes populaires de la Haute Bretagne* (Paris: 1886), p. 74.

8. Françoise Loux et Marie France Morel, "L'Enfance et les savoirs sur le corps. Pratiques médicales et pratiques populaires dans la France traditionelle," *Ethnologie Française* 6, nos. 3-4 (1976), p. 309.

9. J. L. Fourcroy de Guillerville, *Les Enfants élevés dans l'ordre de la nature* (Paris: 1774), p. 80.

10. Archives Nationales, F[17] 9307.

11. Similarly, the inspector from the Oise reported that despite the relative wealth of his department, the scarce population resulted in no interest in establishing schools. Archives Nationales, F[17] 9308.

12. The inspector from the Oise reported that straw huts were sometimes used as schools, and furniture frequently consisted of cabaret tables, smoky stoves, and dirty cupboards which stored books and food. Sometimes the lack of chairs forced pupils to stand throughout the class. Archives Nationales, F[17] 9308. For the Vaucluse, see Mary Jo Maynes, "The Virtues of Archaism: The Political Economy of Schooling," *Comparative Studies of Society and History*, 21, no. 4 (1979), pp. 611-625.

13. Archives Nationales, F[17] 9308.

14. Archives Nationales, F[17] 9309.

15. Archives Nationales, F[17] 9308.

16. Archives Nationales, F[17] 9309.

17. Archives Nationales, F[17] 9310.

18. Archives Nationales, F[17] 9320.

19. Ibid.

20. Baron Dupin, *Forces productives et commerciales de la France,* cited in Fleury and Valmary, "Les Progrès de l'instruction élémentaire de Louis LIV à Napoléon III d'après l'enqûete de Louis Maggiolo (1877-79)," *Population* 12 (1957), p. 293.

21. Ibid.

22. See also Robert Coles, " 'Oh Happy English Children' Coal, Class, and Education in the North-East," *Past and Present* 73 (1976), p. 90.

Lucy Larcom, *A New England Girlhood* (New York: 1889).

René Boudard, "Ecoles d'autrefois: L'Enseignement primarie clandestin dans le départment de la Creuse," *Mémoires de la Société Naturelles et architecturelles de la Creuse* 33, no. 3 (1950).

23. John E. Talbott, "The History of Education," *Daedalus*, vol. 100, 1971, p. 141.

24. In another context, Jack Goody and Ian Watt point out, "In oral societies, the cultural tradition is transmitted almost entirely by face-to-face communication; and changes in its content are accompanied by the homeostatic process of forgetting or transforming those parts of the tradition that cease to be either necessary or relevant. Literate societies . . . are faced with permanently recorded versions of the past and its beliefs; and because the past is thus set apart from the present, historical enquiry becomes possible. This in turn encourages skepticism." J. R. Goody, ed., *Literacy in Traditional Societies* (Cambridge: Cambridge Univerity Press 1968), p. 67.

Two: The ABCs of the Guizot System

1. Abbé Fleury, *Petit Catéchisme historique* (Lyon: 1816), pp. 53-55.
2. *Projet de Loi sur l'instruction primaire,* Jan. 1833, p. 3.
3. *Réglement pour les écoles primaires de la ville de la Croix-Rousse* (Lyon: 1838).
4. T. H. Barrau, *De l'Amour filiale, leçons et récits addressés à la jeunesse* (Paris: 1836), p. 36.
5. A. Antoine de St.-Gervais, *Le Moraliste du jeune âge* (Rouen: 1835), p. 1-11.
6. Laura Strumingher, "L'Ange de la Maison, *International Journal of Women's Studies* 2, no. 1 (Jan.-Feb., 1979), pp. 51-61.
7. Mme. Bourdon, pseud. Mathilde Lippens, *La Vie Réelle* (Paris: 1858), p. 189.
8. Julie Gourand, *Le Livre de Maman* (Paris, 1872), pp. 8, 150, 225, 264.
9. Georges Bruno, pseud. Mme. A. Fouillée, *Francinet* (Paris: 1869).
10. J. M. Dalimier, *La Pédagogie des écoles rurales* (Rennes: 1843), esp. chapters one and two.
11. Gontard, *Ecoles Normales des Institutrices* (Toulouse: n.d.), p. 45.
12. op. cit, Dalimier, ch. 2.
13. Chanoine Jean-Baptiste Ponceau, *Manuel de l'instituteur et de l'institutrice pour la partie morale et religieuse de l'enseignement primaire,* 1856, p. 128.
14. Ibid., p. 129.
15. Ibid., p. 116.
16. Louis Peigné, *La Récitation à l'école* (Paris: 1916³), p. 8.
17. Ibid., p. 16.

Three: Overcoming Parental Opposition to Education

1. Archives Nationales, F¹⁷ 9320.
2. Archives Nationales, F¹⁷ 9370.
3. Archives Nationales, F¹⁷ 10805.

4. Eugen Weber, "Who Sang the Marseillaise?" in Beauroy, Bertrand & Gargon, ed. *Popular Culture in France* (Stanford: 1976, p. 164.

5. Archives Nationales, F^{17} 2649.

6. Weber (above, note 4), p. 166.

7. Eugen Weber, "The Third Republic Makes a Modern Nation," in M. Allain and G. Conrad, ed., *France and North America: Over 300 Years of Dialogue* (Lafayette, Louisiana: 1973), p. 93.

8. Girls in the Limousine who were never sent to school were taught by their mothers how to count and multiply very well. They could rapidly calculate: "Five dozen eggs at 14 sous for one, equals three francs, 10 sous." André Magnoux, "L'Enfance dans nos campagnes limousines d'autrefois," *Lemouzi* 67 (1978), p. 184.

9. Paul Lorain, *Tableau de l'instruction primaire en France* (Paris: 1837), p. 144.

10. Ibid., p. 147.

11. Archives Nationales, F^{17} 12203.

12. Archives Nationales, F^{17} 9368.

13. Archives Nationales, F^{17} 9370.

14. Eugen Weber, "Who Sang the Marseillaise?" in Beauroy et al, ed., *The Wolf and the Lamb: Popular Culture in France from the Old Regime to the Twentieth Century,* Saratoga, 1976.

15. Archives Nationales, F^{17} 10805.

16. Gontard, *Les Ecoles primaires de la France bourgeoise (1833-75)* (Toulouse: n.d.), p. 121.

17. A. Dansette, *Religious History of Modern France,* vol. I (New York, N.Y.: 1961), p. 231.

18. A. Cobban, "The Influence of the Clergy and the Instituteurs Primairies in the Election of the French Constituent," *English Historical Review 57* (1942), p. 349.

19. Gontard, (above, note 16), p. 136.

20. Ibid., p. 159. In 1863, 3,892 took the exam and 2,191, or 56 percent, passed.

21. Ibid., p. 144.

22. E. Keller, *Les Congrégations religieuses en France, leurs oeuvres et leurs services* (Paris, 1880, pp. 710-712.

23. Ibid., pp. 610-611.

24. Julien Clavel, *Histoire de l'école normale d'institutions de Grenoble,* (Grenoble: 1969), p. 44.

Four: The Contribution of Zulma Carraud

1. Romain Guignard, *Balzac et Issoudon* (Issoudon: 1949), p. 22.

2. Archives Nationales, F^{17} 12431, Institutions et pensions des jeunes filles, 1847.

3. Honoré de Balzac, *Correspondance avec Zulma Carraud,* Marcel Bouton, ed., (Paris, 1934).

4. Ibid., p. 96.

5. Ibid., p. 218.

6. *La Ruche journal d'étude familières,* June-July 1848, p. 334.

7. Archives Départementales du Cher, 6T, 197.

8. Archives Hachette generously provided this information.

9. *Livres scolaires en usage dans les écoles primairies publiques,* 1890.

10. See *Bibliothèque scolaire,* list of books recommended by Minister of Public Instruction and Beaux-Arts (Paris: 1891), p. 87.

See also, endorsements by religious authorities on frontispiece of *La Petite Jeanne* and *Maurice,* e.g.

Nous, Charles-Frederic Rousselet, par la miséricorde divine et l'autorité du Saint-Siège apostolique, Evêque de Seez, avons fait examiner le livre intitulé: *Maurice ou le travail.* Sur le rapport que nous en a été fait, nous approvons ledit ouvrage aux mêmes titres qu'un autre de même auteur, apprové par nous, et intitulé: *La Petite Jeanne ou le devoir.* On y trouve les même qualités, le même esprit religieux et le même dévouement de la part de l'auteur au bienêtre des personnes auxquelles est destinés son travail.

11. Patricia Branca, "Image and Reality: The Myth of the Idle Victorian Woman," in Banner and Hartman, eds., *Clio's Consciousness Raised* (New York, 1974).

12. Books written by Zulma Carraud and published in Paris by Hachette that are listed in the Bibliothèque Nationale guide:

1) *Les Goûters de la Grand-mère,* 1868, 2d edition 1869, 3d edition 1879.

2) *Historiettes à l'usage des jeunes enfants qui commencent à savoir lire,* 1853.

3) *Contes et historiettes à l'usage des jeunes enfants qui commencent à savoir lire,* 3d edition 1859, 23 reprints of this work between 1860 and 1898.

4) *Cuentecillos e Historetas para los ninos que empiezan a leer,* 1878, 2d edition 1884, 3d edition 1885, 4th edition 1886, 5th edition 1895.

5) *Historiettes véritables pour les enfants de quatre à huit ans,* 1864, six reprintings from 1866 to 1896.

6) *Lettres de familles, ou modèles de style épistolaire pour les circonstances ordinaires de la vie,* 1855, five reprints from 1858 to 1900.

7) *Le Livre des jeunes filles, simple correspondance,* 1867.

8) *Maurice ou le travail,* 1853, reprinted 32 times from 1854 to 1897.

9) *Les Métamorphoses d'eau,* 1865 2d edition, reprinted once in 1883.

10) *La Petite Jeanne,* 1851, reprinted 41 times from 1851 to 1901.

11) *Une Servante d'autrefois,* 1866, 2d edition in 1869, 3d in 1879, 4th in 1884.

12) *Les Veillés de Maître Patrigeon,* 1868, 2d edition in 1869, 3d in 1873, 4th in 1879, 5th in 1886.

13. Laura S. Strumingher, "La Contribution de Zulma Carraud à la socialization des enfants rurales du dix-neuvième siècle aux rôles masculins/féminin," *Revue de l'académie du centre (forthcoming)*.

Nine: The Children Speak

1. See Margaret Mead, *Culture and Commitment* (New York, N.Y.: 1970), for discussion of co-figurative cultures.
2. Thomas W. Laquer, *Religion and Respectability: Sunday Schools and Working Class Culture* (Yale: 1976), p. 241.
3. See Jay Mechling, "Advice to Historians on Advice to Mothers," *Journal of Social History* 9, 1, pp. 45-63.
4. A. J. T. Pinet, *Les Recreations de l'ecole: Livre pratique de lecture a l'usage des ecoles de filles* (Paris: 1872), pp. 95-96.

Pinet defines *education* as, "the teaching of duties . . . [those] who have the ideas of duties appropriate to their age have the qualities of filial piety, respect, and devotion . . . instruction can never take the place of education, while education can often replace missing instruction," p.99, 100. Cf. *The Royal School Series Domestic Economy,* Third Year Course, used 1850-1910, p. 127: "Above all things, the good manager will know of a surety that her domestic economy cannot be practiced unless she be a keeper at home. She will know that if she employ her time in a factory or a workroom of any kind, or even in the home of some other person, the health, the prosperity and the happiness of her own household, will be put in great danger, if not entirely sacrificed."

5. Luc Boltanski, *Prime Education et morale de classe* (Paris: Mouton, 1969), pp. 33-34.
6. Ibid., p. 70-72.
7. All the material from pupils' notebooks comes from a collection of·400 primary schools notebooks (1786-1914) at the Institut National de Recherche Pédagogique in Mont St Aignan, with the exception of Louis Massot, which is in a private collection in Brive.
8. T. H. Barrau, pseud. for Louis D'Altemont, *Des Devoirs des enfants vers leurs parents* (Paris: 1837), pp. 56-38.
9. T. H. Barrau, *Livre de moral pratique* (Paris: 1849), pp. 360-362, 364-370; A. E. deSaintes, *L'Ange de la Maison* (Paris: 1842).
10. Cf. P. Besson, *Un Patre dans le Cantal* (Paris: 1917, reedited Delagrave 1970).
11. Archives Municipales de Lyon, R¹, Procès-Verbal de la distribution solennelle des prix aux élèves des écoles communales de la ville de Lyon, 1840.

12. Ibid, parish of St. Georges, 1837-1843.
13. ArchivesMunicipales de Lyon, Actes de mariages, Croix-Rousse, 1856, 1866, 1876, 1886.
14. See also the story of Adèle Bellin in my "The Artisan Family: Traditions and Transition in Nineteenth Century Lyon," *Journal of Family History* (Autumn 1977), V. 2, pp. 211-222.
15. Jacques Ozouf, *Nous les maîtres d'école* (Paris: 1967), p. 64.

Ten: Conclusion

1. Eugénie Niboyet, *Le Vrai Livre de femmes* (Paris: 1863), pp. 25-26.

Bibliography

I. ARCHIVAL SOURCES

A. NATIONAL ARCHIVES, Paris

F^{17}

1481	9350-9352	10333
2456-2473	9367-9372	10408-10719
2505	9373-9374	10801-10838
2649-2650	9744-9759	11000-11002
8753-8784	9813-9819	11576-11577
8785-8789	10142-10340	11651-11657
8800-8807	10288	11652
9251-9278	10289	12203
9279-9285	10299	12431-12434
9286-9305	10317	12451-12504
9306-9320	10332	12527
9321-9349		
H 36, 37, 46, 48, 50		

B. MUNICIPAL ARCHIVES, Brive, Bourge, Lyon
R^1 series - schools

C. NATIONAL HISTORICAL MUSEUM OF EDUCATION, Mont Saint Aignan

II. CHILDREN'S BOOKS (1830-1880)

Amis, Sophie. *Les Histoires vraies*. Paris: 1880.
Antoine de St. Gervais, Amboise. *Le Moraliste du jeune âge*. Rouen: 1835.
Arnoul, A. *Au Village. Scènes de la vie rurale*. Paris: 1875.

—— *M. Marcel ou l'ami de la jeunesse.* Paris: 1871.

Aulard, A. *Premières leçons de lecture courante.* Paris: 1873.

—— *Deuxième leçons de lecture courante.* Paris: 1876.

Bader, L. *Syllabaire et premier livre de lecture de l'école premier publique de Mulhouse.* 6e ed., Mulhouse: 1858.

Barrau, T. H. (pseud. for Louis d'Altemont).*Choix de pòesies propres à être apprises par coeur dans les écoles et dans les classes élémentaires des lycées et collèges.* Paris: 1858.

—— *Conseils aux ouvriers sur les moyens qu'ils ont d'être heureux avec l'explication des lois qui les concernent particulièrement.* Paris: 1850.

—— *De l'Amour filial, leçons et récits adressés à la jeunesse.* Paris: 1836.

—— *De l'Éducation dans la famille et au collège.* Paris: 1852.

—— *De l'Éducation morale de la jeunesse.* Paris: 1852

—— *De Devoirs des enfants envers leurs parents.* Paris: 1837.

—— *Direction morale pour les instituteurs.* Paris: 1840

—— *Direction morale pour les instituteurs.* Paris: 1841

—— *Du Rôle de la famille dans l'éducation.* Paris: 1841.

—— *Félix ou le jeune cultivateur: Livre de lecture courante à l'usage des écoles rurales.* Paris: 1868.

—— *Histoire de la révolution française, 1789-1799.* Paris: 1857.

—— *Livre de morale pratique ou choix de préceptes et de beaux exemples, destiné à la lecture courante dans les écoles et les familles.* Paris: 1849.

—— *Loi sur l'enseignement.* Paris: 1853.

—— *Nouvelle loi sur l'enseignement.* Paris: 1850.

Bassanville, Comtesse de., Mme. Anaïs Lebrun. *L'Auxiliaire des mères et des institutrices.* Paris: 1862.

—— *Conseils aux enfants du peuple.* Paris: 1852

—— *De L'Education des femmes.* Paris: 1861.

—— *Les Deux familles - Bonne et mauvaise éducation.* Tours: 1859.

—— Ed., *Le Dimanche des familles.* Paris: 1858.

—— Ed., *La Famille, journal illustré de la mode et de la vie domestique.* 2 vol. Paris: 1ère année, 1868.

—— *La Jeune fille chez tous les peuples: Études morales.* Paris: 1861.

—— Ed., *Journal des jeunes filles.* Paris: 1849-50.

—— *Les Mémoires d'une jeune fille.* Paris: 1849.

—— Ed., *Le Moniteur des demoiselles.* Formerly *Journal des jeunes filles.* Paris: 1851-52, 1853-54.

—— *Du Perfectionnement de l'éducation des filles.* Paris: 1847.

—— *Les Salons d'autrefois, souvenirs intimes.* Préface de Louis Enault. Paris: 1862-1866.

—— *Les Secrets d'une jeune fille.* Paris: 1863.

—— *Souvenirs d'une douairière.* Paris: 1868.

Beaumont, Mme. le Prince de. *Le Magasin des enfants ou Dialogues d'une sage gouvernante avec ses élèves de la première distinction, dans lesquels on fait penser, etc.* 2 vol., 1758.

Belèze, M. Guillaume-Louis-Gustave. *Dictée et lectures.* Paris: 1854, 1869.
——— *Livre de lecture courante.* Paris: 1852.
——— *Nouveau cours d'enseignement élémentaire.* Paris: 1854–1886.
——— *Premières lectures à l'usage des écoles primaires.* Paris: 1875.
Belloc, Mme. Louise Swanton. *Pierre et Pierrette: Dangers de vagabondage.* Paris: 1838.
Bernardin, Frère. *Le Syllabaire.* Paris. 1848.
Berranger, L'Abbé. *Syllabaire et livre de lecture à l'usage des écoles chrétiennes.* Paris: 1861.
Bertaut, Mme. Léonie. *Le Livre de mes enfants: Lectures à l'usage des écoles primaires et des établissements secondaires des jeunes filles.* Paris: 1886.
Besson, Pierre. *Un Pâtre du Cantal.* Paris: 1917 2nd edition, 1970.
Boniface, A. *Une Lecture par jour.* Paris: 1863.
Bonnier, Mlle. *Le Bonheur des enfants. Lectures pour le jeune âge.* Paris: 1869.
Bourdon, Mme. (Pseud. for Mathilde Lippens, dame Froment; later pseud. Mathilde Tarwelg). *Les Legs d'une mère.* Lille: 1851.
——— *Les Mères reconciliées par leurs enfants.* Drame. Paris: 1853.
——— *Les Souvenirs d'une institutrice.* Paris: 1859.
Bruno, G. (pseud. for Mme. Alfred Fouillée, 1833–1923). *Francinet.* Paris: 1869.
Caillard, Mme. Paul. *Entretiens familiers d'une institutrice avec six élèves. Essai de méthode pratique sur l'éducation, spécialement destiné aux écoles primaires.* Paris: 1863.
——— *Petit cours de leçons morales et pratiques, à l'usage des jeunes enfants dans les salles d'asile et les écoles communales.* Paris: 1865.
——— *Robert l'apprenti ou l'histoire interrompue, petite civilité en action.* Paris: 1880.
Calendrini. *Récits moraux à l'usage des salles d'asiles.* Paris: 1838.
Campan, Jeanne-Louise-Henriette Genest, Dame. *Conseils aux jeunes filles. Paris: 1825.*
——— *Correspondance inédite de Mme. Campan avec la reine Hortense de Holland.* 2 vols. Paris: 1835.
——— *De l'Education.* 2 vols. Paris: 1824.
——— *Journal anecdotique.* Paris: 1824.
——— *Lettres de deux jeunes amies, élèves d'Ecouen.* Paris: 1824.
——— *Soirées d'Ecouen.* Recueillies et publiées par Stéphanie Ory. Paris: 1880.
Carraud, Mme. (Mme. Zulma Touranger, veuve). *Les Goûters de la grand-mère.* Paris: 1868.
——— *Historiettes vétiables pour les enfants de 4 a 8 ans.* Paris: 1864.
——— *Le Livre des jeunes filles, simple correspondance.* Paris: 1867.
——— *Maurice ou le travail.* Paris: 1853
——— *Les Métamorphoses d'une goutte d'eau.* Paris: 1864.
——— *La Petite Jeanne ou le devoir.* Paris: 1852.
——— *Une Servante d'autrefois.* Paris: 1866.
——— *Les Veillées de maître Patrigeon.* Paris: 1868.

Caumont. *Lectures courantes des écoliers francais. La Famille, la maison. Le Village. Notre pays.* 2 vol Paris: 1880.

—— *Lectures courantes des écoliers francais.* Paris: 1876.

Chaumeil. *Lectures alternées sur l'éducation, l'instruction et l'économie domestique à l'usage des familles et des écoles de filles.* Paris: 1878.

Chevreau-Lemercier, Mme. *Petites histoires pour les enfants des salles d'asiles.* Paris: 1865.

Delapalme. *Premiers lectures dans les manuscrites à l'usage des écoles primailres.* Paris: 1873.

DeSaintes, A. E. (pseud. de Eymery, Alexis). *Thérèse ou la petite soeur de charité.* Paris: 1833.

—— *Les Avantages de l'éducation. Adeline et Virginie.* Paris: 1877.

—— *L'Ange de la maison.* Paris: 1842.

—— *Les Délassements de ma fille.* Paris: 1830.

Dupont, H. A. *Leçons de choses: Récits enfantins.* Paris: 1881.

Fabre, J. Henri. *Le Ménage; causeries d'Aurore avec ses nièces sur l'économie domestique.* Paris: 1880.

—— *Les Petites filles.* Premier livre de lecture à l'usage des écoles primaires. Paris: 1878.

Falaize, Caroline Jacquemain, Mme. *Confidences d'une jeune fille.* Paris: 1880.

—— *Leçons d'une mère à ses enfants sur la religion.* 2 vols. Paris: 1836.

Faucon, Emma. *Cendrillon.* Paris: 1862.

—— *Lettres d'une jeune fille à sa mère.* Paris: 1865.

—— *Voyage d'une jeune fille autour de sa chambre.* Paris: 1860.

Gourand, Julie. *Le livre de maman.* Paris: 1872.

Guillemot, J. *La Semaine de l'enfant.* Premier livre de lecture à l'usage des écoles primaires. 5e ed. Paris: 1872.

Guizot, Pauline. *Les Enfants, contes à l'usage de la jeunesse.* 2 vol. Paris: N.D., 3e ed. 1824.

Henriot. *Choix de lectures pour l'année.* Paris: 1867.

Hébert-Duperon, l'abbé Victor. *Premier livre de l'école et de la famille.* Paris: 1867.

Juranville, Mlle. Cl. *Le Premier livre des petites filles.* Paris: 1873.

—— *Le Deuxième livre des petites-filles.* Paris: 1887.

Jussieu, L.P. de. *Histoires et causeries morales et instructives à l'usage des jeunes filles chrétiennes.* Paris: 1856.

—— *Histoire de Charlotte Champion ou Mère Séraphique.* Paris: 1851.

—— *Oeuvres posthumes de Simon de Nantua, recueillies par son ancien compagnon de voyage.* Paris: 1829.

—— *Simon de Nantau ou le marchand forain.* Paris: 1817.

Lajolais, Nathalie de. *Le livre des mères de familles et des institutrices.* Paris: 1841.

Larousse, Pierre and Alfred Deberle. *Les Jeudis de l'institutrice. Livre de lecture courante à l'usage des pensionats de demoiselles de 12 a 18 ans.* Paris: N.D.

Lebrun, Elise. *Le Volu de la petite Jeanne*. Paris: 1893.

Lemaire. H. *Modèles de la jeunesse ou nouvelles histoires composées pour l'instruction et l'amusement des deux sexes*. Paris: 1827.

Le Mare, P. A. *Cours de lecture consistent en 68 figures et 48 contes*. Paris: 1840.

Lorain, Paul. *Tableau de l'instruction primaire en France d'après des documents authentiques*. Paris: 1837.

Martin de Noirlieu. (Abbé François). *La Bible de l'enfance à l'histoire abrégée de l'Ancien et du Nouveau Testament, racontée aux enfants de huit à douze ans*. 3 vol. Paris: 1839.

Massieu, Mme. de. *La Vraie politesse*. Paris: 1846.

Méchin, L'Abbé. F. *Fleurs et épines ou vertus et défauts*. Paris: 1866.

Monniot, Victorine. *Le Journal de Marguerite ou deux années préparatoires à la première communion*. 2 vol. Paris: 1858.

——— *Marguerite a vingt ans. Suite et fin du journal de Marguerite*. Paris: 1861.

——— *Madame Roséfly ou la marâtre chrétienne*. 2 vol. Paris: 1864.

——— *Nina l'incorrigible, ou la première confession*. Paris: 1863.

——— *Notre Seigneur, Jésus Christ. Etudes et méditations pour les jeunes filles*. Paris: 1874.

——— *La Petite Concierge*. Paris: 1872.

——— *Les Petites filles de Mme. Roséfly*. 2 vol. Paris: 1880.

——— *Simples tableaux d'éducation maternelle et chrétienne*. 2 vol. Paris: 1870.

Niaudet, F. A. *Un Peu de tout ce qu'il est bon de savoir*. Dijon: 1868.

Niboyet, Eugénie. *Des Aveugles et de leur éducation*. Paris: 1873.

——— *Contes moraux, dédiées à la jeunesse des écoles*. Paris: 1879.

——— *Les Deux frères*. Paris: 1879.

——— *Les Leçons pour les petits enfants*. 2 vols., Paris: 1836.

——— *Petits contes pour les enfants de 4–5 ans*. Paris: 1836.

——— *Souvenirs d'enfance*. Paris: 1841.

——— *Le Vrai livre des femmes*. Paris: 1863.

Pape-Carpentier, Marie. *Conseils sur la direction des salles d'asile*. Paris: 1846.

——— *Enseignement pratique dans les écoles maternelles*. Paris: 1849.

——— *Histoire naturelle. Leçons préparatoires à l'étude de l'hygiène*. Editions, garçons. Paris: 1870. Editions, filles. Paris: 1870.

——— *Lectures et travail pour les enfants et les mères*. Paris: 1872.

Pichard, Mlle. Lilla. *La Bonne petite fille ou l'enfant et ses devoirs*. Paris: 1872.

——— *Le Journal d'une femme de bien*. Paris: 1881.

——— *Madame Adéline — Récits d'une institutrice à ses élèves sur l'intelligence des animaux*. Paris: 1867.

Pinet, Mme. A. J. T. *Les Récréations de l'école; Livre pratique de lecture à l'usage des écoles de filles*. Paris: 1872.

Rapat, J. J. *Cours d'études des écoles primaires*. Paris: 1860.

Ravaisson, Félix. *De l'Habitude*. Paris: 1838.

Rendu, Ambroise. *L'Economie politique à l'école primaire: Petit manuel pratique*. Paris: 1880.

Richomme, Fanny., ed. *Les Beautés de l'âme, livre des jeunes filles par divers auteurs, sous la direction de Mme. F. R.* Paris: 1847.

Savignac, Alida. *L'Economie domestique ou conseils à la jeunesse industrieuse.* 2 vol. Paris: 1828

—— *Encouragements donnés à la jeunesse industrieuse.* 2 vol. Paris: 1828

—— *Pauline ou la petite curieuse.* Paris: 1835.

Segalas, Anaïs. *Enfantines, poésies à ma fille.* Paris: 1844.

—— *La Femme, poésies.* Paris: 1847

—— *Les Mariages dangereux.* Paris: 1878.

Stelley, F. *Lectures pour les petites filles.* Tours: 1903.

Tastu, Amiable. *Education maternelle; simples leçons d'une mère à ses enfants.* Paris: 1869.

—— *Le Livre des femmes, choix de morceaux extraits de meilleurs écrivains français sur la caractère, les moeurs et l'esprit des femmes.* Paris: 1823.

—— *Les Récits du maître d'école, lectures pour l'enfance, ou l'adolescent conduit à la virtu, au savoir et à l'industrie.* Paris: 1844, 1880.

Thery, Augustin F. *Conseils aux mères.* Deuxième partie. Paris: 1837.

Wirth, Ernestine. *Le Livre de lecture courante des jeunes filles chrétiennes.* Paris: 1870.

III. TEACHER'S GUIDES

A. BOOKS

Badin, E. *Qu'a-t-on fait et que veut-on faire pour l'enseignement primaire.* Paris: N. D.

Berger-Brouard, Dafodon. *Manuel d'examen pour le brevet de capacité de l'enseignement primailre à l'usage des aspirants et des aspirantes au brevet élémentaire.* Paris: 1874.

Berthon, Inspecteur primaire à Lyon. *De L'Enseignement de la lecture courante dans les écoles primaires.* (Conférence pédagogique le 7 Dec. 1877). Paris: 1878.

Buisson, F. *Dictionnaire de pédagogie et d'instruction primaire.* Paris: 1878.

Catillion, Le. R. P., de la Compagnie de Jésus. *Manuel pédagogique de la religieuse enslignante.* Soissons: 1887.

Chabert, E. A. *Guide pratique de l'instituteur et de l'institutrice ou le livre du maître.* 2 vol. Paris: 1873.

Cochin, J. D. M. *Manuel des fondateurs et des directeurs des premiers écoles de l'enfance connues sous le nom de salles d'asile.* Paris: 1853.

Daligault. *Cours pratique de pédagogie destiné aux élèves-maîtres des écoles normales primaires.* Paris: 1851.

Dalimier, J. M. *La Pédagogie des écoles rurales.* Rennes: 1843.

Delasiauve, Louis Jean François.   *Nature et dégré de l'enseignement qu'il convient de donner dans les écoles primaires.* Paris: 1849.

Dezobry et Magdaline.   *De l'Examen des livres scolaires au ministère de l'instruction publique.* Paris: 1853.

Dumouchel, J. F. A.   *Leçons de pédagogie. Conseils relatifs à l'éducation et à l'enseignement dans les écoles primaires.* Paris: 1850.

Forneron, J. B.   *Guide des instituteurs ou principes de pédagogie pour l'instruction primaire.* Paris: 1851.

Hébert-Duperon, L'Abbe Victor.   *Conseils aux institutrices.* Paris: 1865.

——   *Souvenirs des distributions des prix.* Paris: 1865.

Jacquot, F.   *Le Bon maître d'école au 19e siècle avec les méthodes touloises, allemandes, chinoises, arabes, et françaises pour l'enseignement élémentaire.* Paris: 1858.

Lévi-Alvarès, David E.   *La Mère Institutrice.* Paris: 1836.

——   *Livres Scolaires en usage dans les écoles primaires publiques.* Musée Pédagogique, Paris: 1890.

Mansion, H. L.   *Le Petit Rollin. Traité des études primaires. Cours de pédagogie.* Paris: 1851

Maréchal, Fanny.   *Conseils aux mères pour la première éducation du coeur.* Paris: 1850.

Marlotti.   *Conférences normales de pédagogie. Manuel des élèves-maîtres et des instituteurs.* 3 vol. Paris: 1868.

Martin, Henri.   *Précis de pédagogie catéchistique.* Paris: 1934.

——   *Manuel de l'instituteur pour les élections.* Paris: 1848.

Matter, Jacques.   *L'Instituteur primaire ou conseils et directions pour préparer les instituteurs à leurs carrières et les diriger dans l'exercise de leurs fonctions.* Paris: 1843.

Meissas, Texte.   *Manuel d'examen pour le brevet de capacité d'enseignement primaire conforme à la loi de 1850 et Février 1853, à l'usage des aspirants et des aspirantes.* 2 vol. Paris: 1860-1863.

Petetin, Abbé François. Curé d'Arinthod (Jura).   *L'Institutrice au village ou manuel de l'institutrice.* Lons-le-Saunier: 1863.

Pidoux, P.   *L'Education populaire. Conseils aux institutions sur la direction à · donner à leur enseignement.* Le Puy: 1866.

Pinet, Bravard, et Mattas.   *Manuel de l'instituteur primaire ou résumé des conférences faite aux instituteurs du Loiret.* Paris: 1855.

Ponceau, Jean Baptiste, J. H. Chanoine.   *Manuel de l'instituteur et de l'institutrice pour la partie morale et religieuse de l'enseignement primaire.* Paris: 1856.

Rendu, Ambroise.   *Cours de pédagogie ou principes d'éducation publique à l'usage des élèves des écoles normales et des instituteurs primaires.* Paris: 1845.

——   *Essai sur l'instruction publique et particulierèment sur l'instruction primaire.* Paris: 1819.

——— *Récits moraux et instructif livre de lecture à l'usage des écoles primaires.* Paris: 1857.

Sauvan, Mlle. Jeanne-Lucille. *Cours normal des institutrices primaire.* Paris: 1840.

Savignac, Alida de. *Adrienne, ou les conseils d'une institutrice.* Tours: 1847.

Théry, Augustin. *Lettres sur la profession d'instituteur.* Paris: 1853.

——— *Lettres sur la profession d'institutrice.* Paris: 1869.

B. JOURNALS

Bulletin de la ligue de l'enseignement (depuis 1868).

L'Echo des instituteurs. 1845-1851.

L'Emancipation de l'enseignement. 1848-1851

Journal des instituteurs. 1858-1931.

Journal des mères et des jeunes filles. 1844-1847.

Manuel général de l'instruction primaire: Journal mensuel. 1858-1864.

Petit manuel de l'instruction primaire: Journal mensuel des instituteurs. 1854-1864.

Revue de l'enseignement des femmes. 1845-1848.

Revue de l'instruction publique. 1842-1870.

IV. GENERAL EDUCATION SOURCES

Alfaric, P. *Jean Macé, fondateur de la ligue française de l'enseignement.* Paris: 1955.

Ancelot-Hustache, Jeanne. *Les Dames de Calvaires.* Paris: 1938.

Anderson, Michael R. *Education in France: 1848-1870.* London: 1975.

Banks, Olive *The Sociology of Education.* New York: 1976.

Barnard, H. C. *Education and the Franch Revolution.* London: 1969.

Baudoin, J. M. *Rapport sur l'état actuel de l'enseignement spécial et de l'enseignement primaire en Belgique, en Allemagne et en Suisse.* Paris: 1965.

Bert, Paul. *Des Conditions du recrutement et du fonctionnement des instituteurs et institutrices primaires.* (Rapport au nom de la commission parlementaire). Paris: May, 1977.

Beugnot, Arthur Auguste. *Rapport fait au nom de la commission chargée d'examiner le projet de loi sur l'instruction publique.* Paris: 1849

Boiraud, Henri. *La Condition féminine et la scolarization des filles en France au XIX siècle.* (Guizot à Ferry). Thèse d'Etat. Caen.

Boltanski, Luc. *Prime éducation et morale de classe.* Paris: 1969.

Bonsirven, P. *Simeon Roucou, Curé de Massac, fondateur des pâtures filles de Jésus.* Toulouse: 1939.

Boudard, Rene.   "L'Enseignement primaire clandestin dans le département de la Creuse entre 1830 et 1880." *Mémoires de la Creuse.* 33 (1959): 525-535.

Boulay de la Meurthe.   (François Joseph, comte, 1799-1880). *Discours à l'ouverture de l'Assemblée Générale de la Société pour l'linstruction élémentaire.* Paris: 1850.

——   *L'Instruction primaire à Paris depuis la révolution de Février.* Paris: 1848.

Bourgain, M. P.   *Octave Gréard. Un moraliste éducateur.* Paris: 1907.

Breal, M.   *Quelques mots sur l'instruction publique en France.* Paris: 1872, 1881.

Brouard, E.   *Essai d'histoire critique de l'instruction primaire en France de 1789 à nos jours.* Paris: 1901.

Brouard, E., and Defodon.   *Inspection des écoles primaires.* Paris: 1878.

Buisson et al.   *La Lutte scolaire en France au XIXe siècle. Leçons professées à l'école des Hautes Etudes Sociales.* Paris: 1912.

Cabrié, Louis.   *Le Guide des écoles de filles.* Toulouse: 1844.

Capéran, L.   *Histoire contemporaine de la laïcite.* Paris: 1957.

Carbonnier, M.   "Une bibliothèque populaire aux XIXe siècle." *Revue Française d'Histoire du Livre.* Paris: July, August, Sept., 1978.

Carnot, Paul.   *Hippolyte Carnot et le ministère de l'instruction publique de la 2eme République.* Paris: 1948.

Cedoz, Abbé.   *Un Couvent de religieuses anglaises à Paris de 1634 à 1884.* Paris: 1891

Cère.   *De L'Enseignement primaire. Les frères de la doctrine chrétienne et les instituteurs laïques.* Paris: 1847.

Chambolle, J.   "L'Enseignement primaire dans l'Isère de 1848-1860. Essai d'histoire sociale de l'école populaire." *DES.* Grenoble: 1959.

Champagny, Le Comte de.   *Lettres sur l'éducation des filles.* Paris: 1879.

Chapelle, F.   *Lectures choisies du premier âge.* Paris: 1871.

Charlot, Bernard.   *La Mystification pédagogique.* Paris: 1977.

Charrier, Edmée.   *L'Evolution intellectuelle féminine.* Paris: 1931.

Chenesseau, G.   *La Commission extraparlementaire de 1849.* Paris: 1937.

Chevalier, Alexis.   *Les Frères des écoles chrétiennes après la révolution 1797-1830.* Paris: 1887.

Chevokjan, L'Abbe.   *Le Manuel de la jeune fille chrétienne.* Paris: 1860.

——   *La Perfection des jeunes filles.* Paris: 1856.

Chieulet, Jean.   *L'Education du peuple en France à travers les âges.* Paris: 1952.

Cipolla, C. M.   *Literary Development in the West.* Harmondsworth: 1969.

Cobban, A.   "The Influence of the Clergy and the Instituteurs primaires in the election of the French Constituante." *English Historical Review.* 57 (1942): pp. 334-344.

Cogniot, Georges.   *La Question scolaire en 1848.* Paris: 1948.

Comité de l'enseignement libre: Commentaire sur la loi d'enseignement du 15 Mars, 1850. Publiée par le Comité de l'enseignement libre, Président M. Le Comte Molé, 1851.

Compayré, Gabriel.   *Histoire critique des doctrines de l'éducation en France depuis le XVIe siècle.* 2 vol. Paris: 1879.

Cuissart, E. "L'Enseignement primaire à Lyon et dans le département du Rhône avant et après 1789," *Revue de Lyonnais*. 4e série, tome IX: 337–346, 430–438, tome X: 7–14, 84–96.

Dansette, A. *Histoire religieuse de la France contemporaine*. Paris: 1948.

Darman, J. J. *Le Colportage de librairie en France sous le Second Empire*. Paris: 1972.

Daubie, J. *Du Progrés dans l'instruction primaire*. Paris: 1862.

Dauriat, Louise. *Demande en révision du code civil addressée aux membres de la Chambre des Députés*. Paris: 1837.

—— *Discours d'ouverture du cours de droit social des femmes, au Ranelagh en séance publique, le 29 Mai, 1836*. Passy: N.D.

D'Avenal, Victor George. "Le Gôut de l'instruction et son prix depuis 3 siècles." *Revue des Deux Mondes*. 4, (1929): pp. 827–859.

De Cormenin, Timon. *L'Education et l'enseignement*. Paris: 1847.

De Girardin, E. *L'Instruction publique en France*. Paris: 1840.

De Laveleye, E. *L'Instruction du peuple*. Paris: 1872.

—— "L"Instruction du peuple au XIXe siècle." *Revue des Deux Mondes*. Paris: 1866.

Delcourt, André. "Les Sociétés fondatrices des écoles primaires libres laïques et gratuites." *Bulletin de l'Institut d'Histoire Sociologique*. April, 1953: 8–21.

Deniel, Raymond. *Une image de la famille et de la société sous la Restauration 1815–30*. Paris: 1965.

Derome, L. *L'Eglise et l'instruction primaire à la campagne*. Paris: 1861.

Dessoye, A. *Défense laïque*. Paris: 1913.

—— *Jean Macé et la ligue de l'enseignement*. Paris: 1883.

—— *L'Enseignement secondaire et la République*. Paris: 1902.

Drouilly, François. *L'Ecole primaire congréganiste dans le département du Rhône (1850–80)*. DES. Lyon: 1965.

Dubuisson, Jane. *Lettres d'un rapin de Lyon à un rapin de Paris*. Lyon: 1837.

—— *Mlle. Magland*. Lyon: 1845.

Du Courtieux, Paul. *L'Instruction dans la Haute-Vienne, 1869–1885*. Limoges: 1886.

Duhaut, J. *Manuel des écoles primaires*. Nancy: 1851.

—— *Le Véritable manuel des écoles primaires; recueil de plus de 1400 problèmes pratiques, relatifs à toutes les professions ordinaires*. Nancy: 1859.

Dumon, P. *De L'Education populaire et des études normales primaires*. Paris: 1841

Dupanloup, Félix. Bishop of Orléans. Abbé et Mgr. *De L'Education en général*. 3 vol. Paris: 1851.

—— *La Femme chrétienne et française*. Paris: 1868.

—— *Femmes savantes et femmes studieuses*. Paris: 1868.

—— *La Femme studieuse*. Paris: 1875.

—— *Lettres sur l'éducation des filles et sur les études qui conviennent aux femmes dans le monde*. Paris: 1907.

—— *M. Duruy et l'éducation des filles*. Paris: 1867.

Dupuy, Aimé. "Histoire sociale et manuels scolaires." *Revue d'Histoire économique et sociale, no.2, 1953.*

Duruy, Victor. *L'Administration et l'instruction publique de 1863 à 1869.* Paris: N.D.

—— *Notes et souvenirs.* 2 vol. Paris: 1901.

Duveau, G. *La Pensée ouvrière sur l'éducation pendant la Seconde République.* Paris: 1948.

—— *Les Instituteurs.* Paris: 1957.

Exposition Internationale Universelle de 1900. Catalogue général officiel. Tome premier. Groupe I. (écoles).

Ezerville, J. J. *Nos bonnes religieuses françaises; leurs états de service dans les classes péndant la guerre de 1871.* Paris: 1878.

Faury, Jean. *Cléricalisme et anti-cléricalisme dans le Tarn.* Toulouse: 1979.

Fleury, M., et P. Valmary. "Le Progrés de l'instruction élémentaire de Louis XIV à Napoléon III d'après l'enquête de Louis Maggiolo 1877-79." *Population* 12, (1957): 71-93.

Fritsche, Joseph. *Discipline à domicile.* Recherche #28, Paris: 1977.

Furet, J. B, *Sentences, leçons, avis du vénéré P. Champagnat expliqués et développés par un de ses premiers disciples.* Paris: 1868.

Gaume, Jean Joseph. *Du Catholicisme dans l'éducation.* Paris: 1835.

Gauthier-Coignet, Clarisse. *Biographie de Mme. Lemonnier, fondatrice de la Société pour l'Enseignement Professionnel des femmes.* Paris: 1866.

—— *De l'Enseignement publique.* Paris: 1856.

—— *La Morale dans l'éducation.* Paris: 1883.

—— *La Morale indépendante.* Paris: 1869.

—— *Rapport présenté à la Commission de l'Enseignement Communal.* Paris: 1870.

—— *Rapport présenté au nom de la Commission des Dames Chargée d'Examiner.* Paris: 1871.

Gavault, Paul. *Les Livres de l'enfance XVe au XIXe Siècles.* 2 vol., N.D.

Gontard, M. *Une Bataille scolaire au XIXe siècle 1869–1873.* Lyon: N.D.

—— *Les Ecoles primaires de la France 1853–1875.* Paris: N.D.

—— *L'Enseignement primaire en France de la révolution à la loi Guizot (1789–1833).* Paris: 1959.

—— *L'Oeuvre scolaire de la 3e république 1876–1914.* Toulouse: N.D.

—— *La question des écoles normales primaires de la révolution de 1789 à nos jours.* Paris: 19621.

Gossot, E. *Essai critique sur l'enseignement primaire en France de 1800 à 1900.* Paris: 1901.

—— *Mme. Marie Pape-Carpentier; sa vie et son oeuvre.* Paris: 1890 and 1894.

—— *Les Salles d'asile en France.* Paris: 1884.

—— *Mlle. Sauvan (Jeanne-Lucille): Première inspectrice des écoles de Paris. Sa Vie et son oeuvre.* Paris: 1860.

Gréard, O. *Education et instruction.* Paris: 1887.

—— *L'Education des femmes par les femmes. Etudes et portraits.* Paris: 1886.

—— *L'Enseignement secondaire des filles.* Paris: 1882.

La Législation de l'instruction primaire en France depuis 1789 jusqu'á nos jours (1874). 3vol., Paris: 1874.

—— *Les Résultats de l'enseignement primaire à Paris de 1867 à 1878.* Orléans: 1879.

Grimaud, Louis. *Histoire de la liberté d'enseignement en France.* Paris: 1944.

Grignard, Romain. *Balzac et Issoudon.* Paris: 1949.

Guilleville, J. L. Fourcroy de. *Les Enfants élevés dans l'ordre de la nature.* Paris: 1774.

Guizot, Pauline. *Lettres de famille sur l'éducation.* 2 vol., Paris: 1774.

Hélot, René. *La Bibliothèque bleu en Normandie.* Rouen: 1929.

Héricourt, Mme. Jenny P. d'. *La Femme affranchie.* Paris: 1860.

—— *Le Fils du reprouvé par Félix Lamb.* Paris: 1844.

Isambert-Jamati, V. *Crises de la société, crises de l'enseignement: Sociologie de l'enseignement secondaire français.* Paris: P.U.F., 1970.

Janicot, J. *Monographie des écoles communales de Lyon depuis 1828 à 1891.* Lyon: 1891.

Jefferson, C. "Worker Education in England and France, 1800-1914." *Comparative Studies in Society and History 6(1964): 345-366.*

Johnson, Richard. "Educational Policy and Social Conflict in Early Victorian England" *Past and Present* 49 (Nov. 1970): 96-119.

Jourdain, Charles. *L'Education des femmes au moyen âge.* Paris: 1871.

—— *Quelques mots sur le rapport de M. Compayré, député; au nom de la commission de la chambre chargée d'examiner les projets relatifs à l'enseignement secondaire libre.* Paris: N.D.

—— *Rapports sur le progrés de l'instruction publique.* Paris: 1867.

Kulstein, D. I. "Economics Instruction for Workers during the Second Empire." *French Historical Studies* vol.I (1959): 225-234.

LaCottière, E. Jacob de. *Quelques réflexions sur l'éducation des filles de la campagne.* Lyon: 1856.

La Farque, G. *Education primaire obligatoire.* Paris: 1867.

Lammenais, J. M. de. *Guide du premier âge.* Paris: 1852.

Landais, N. *De l'Education et de l'instruction en France.* Paris: 1837.

Laquer, Thomas. "English and French Education in the 19th Century" *History of Education Quarterly* (Spring, 1973): 13, pp. 53-60.

—— "Working Class Demand . . . " in Lawrence Stone, ed. *Schooling and Society.* Johns Hopkins Univ. Press, Baltimore, 1976.

Latzarus, Marie-Thérèse. *Littérature enfantine en France pendant le deuxième moitié du XIXe siècle.* Paris: 1923.

Laveleye, F. *L'Instruction supérieure pour les femmes.* Bruxelles: 1882.

Léaud et Glay. *L'Ecole primaire en France.* 2 vol., Paris: 1934.

Leblois, Louis. *La Maison de la femme et son rôle dans l'éducation réligieuse de l'enfance.* Paris: 1865.

Lemoine, René. *L'Enseignement mutuel dans le département de la Somme sous la seconde restauration.* Paris: 1933.

—— *La Loi Guizot. Son application dans le départment de la Somme.* Paris: 1933

L'Enseignement public. Centennaire de Pauline Kergomard. Paris: 1938.

Lévy, Marie-Françoise. "Le Rôle de l'église à travers l'éducation morale et religieuse des femmes en France de 1850-1870." *Mémoire de Maîtrice;* Univ. de Paris VII. June, 1979.

Lougee, Carolyn C. "Noblesse, Domesticity and Agrarian Reform: The Education of Girls by Fenelon and St. Cyr." *History of Education Quarterly* (Spring 1974). 14, 87-111.

Loux, Françoise et Marie-France Morel. "L" Enfance et les savoirs sur le corps. Pratiques médicales et pratiques populaires dans la France traditionelle." *Ethnologie Française, 6, 3-4 (1976): 309-314.*

Luiz, P. *Scènes de la vie d'instituteur.* Paris: 1868.

Magnoux, André. "L'Enfance dans nos campagnes limousines d'autrefois." *Lemouzi 67 (1978): 176-185.*

Malardier, P. *Mission sociale des instituteurs ou l'évangile et la republique.* Paris: 1848.

Martin, Charles. *Lettre sur l'état de l'instruction primaire depuis la promulgation de la loi du 28 Juin, 1833.* Paris: N.D.

Matter, Jacques. *Le visiteur des écoles. 2ᵉ ed., Paris: 1838.*

Maurain, J. *La Politique écclésiastique du Second Empire.* Paris: 1830.

Meunier, L. a. *Le Cours d'adultes de 1837 à 1842. Paris: 1882.*

—— *Défense des institutiurs laïques contre les attaques du clergé.* Paris: 1847.

—— *De l'Enseignement congréganiste.* Paris: 1845.

—— *Du Rôle de la Famille dans l'éducation.* Paris: 1856.

—— *Lettre à M.le Ministre de l'insruction publique sur les besoins actuels de l'instruction primaire dans les campagnes.* Paris: 1861.

—— *Lutte du principe clérical et du principe laïque dans l'enseignement.* Paris: 1861.

Michel, H. *La Loi Falloux.* Paris: 1906.

Mistler, Jean. *Hachette, cent cinquante d'édition.* Paris: 1976.

Mond, Louis. *Le Droit d'enseignement. Ecoles laïques et écoles congréganistes.* Lyon: 1878.

Morin, Arthur Jules. *France: Commission de l'enseignement professionnel.* Paris: 1865.

Necker de Saussure, Mme. *Education progressive ou étude de cours de la vie.* Paris: 1828.

Niderst. *L'Enseignement primaire en France.* Strasbourg: 1935.

Oberle, R. and P. Leuilliot. "L'Enseignement au XIXᵉ siècle et l'histoire sociale." *Comité des travaux historiques et scientifiques. Bulletin de la section d'histoire moderne et contemporaine.* Tome IV, 1962, 25-39.

D'Ollendon, M. E. *Bibliographie de l'enseignement primaire.* Paris: 1878-88.

Ozouf, J. *Nous les maîtres d'ecole. Autobiographies d'instituteurs de la belle époque.* Paris: 1967.

—— "Le Thème du patriotisme dans les manuels primaires." *Le Mouvement Social* 49 (Oct.-Dec. 1964): 5-31.

Paradis, Ernest. *L'Enseignement congréganiste et ses conséquences funestes.* Paris: 1868.

Pecaut, Félix. "Ecole normale de Fonteray-aux-roses." *Revue de l'Enseignement Primaire.* May 23, 1897, 279.

Pichenot, Mgr. Archévêque de Chambery. *Traité pratique de l'éducation maternelle.* Paris: 1878.

Piette, E. *De l'Education du peuple.* Paris: 1859.

Plane, J. *L'Enseignement dans une école primaire.* Clermont-Ferrand: 1868.

—— *La Gratuite absolue de l'enseignement primaire.* Thiers: 1870.

Pouthas, D. H. *Démocraties et capitalismes 1848-1860.* Paris: 1948.

Prost, Antoine. *L'Enseignement en France, 1800-1967.* Paris: 1968.

Querrien, Anne. *L'Enseignement: L'Ecole primaire.* Recherches 23. June 1976.

Raphael. "Les Recteurs de 1850" *Revue d'Histoire Moderne.* 1935. 10, pp. 448-487.

Remeusat, Claire de. *Essai sur l'éducation des femmes.* Paris: 1824.

Rendu, Ambroise. *De l'Association charitable des frères des écoles chrétiennes.* Paris: 1845.

—— *De l'Enseignement obligatoire.* Paris: 1853.

—— *L'Instruction primaire devant l'Assemblée Nationale.* Paris: 1873.

—— *Lettres à un instituteur primaire sur les droits et les devoirs du citoyen.* Paris: 1848.

—— *De la loi de l'enseignement. Commentaire théorique et administratif.* Paris: 1850.

—— *L'Obligation légale de l'enseignement.* Paris: 1871.

Renouvier, Ch. *Manuel républicain de l'homme et du citoyen.* Paris: 1848.

Rivaux, Jean-Joseph. *Vie de Mère Saint-Jean Fontbonne.* Grenoble: 1885.

Rivet, José. *Les Oeuvres de charité et les établissements d'enseignement libre de 1789-1945.* Paris and Lyon: 1945.

Robert, Charles. *De l'Ignorance des populations ouvrières et rurales en France.* Montbéliard: 1863.

—— *De la Nécessité de rendre l'instruction primaire obligatoire.* Montbéliard: 1861.

—— *L'Instruction obligatoire.* Paris: 1871.

—— *Plaintes et voeux présentés par les instituteurs publiques en 1861 sur la situation des maisons d'écoles du mobilier et du matériel classique.* Paris: 1864.

Roselly de Lorgues. *Le Livre des communes ou régénération de la France.* Paris: 3ᵉ ed., 1842.

Rosen-Dufaure, Sophie. *L'Education devant le dogme ancien et la philosophie moderne.* Conférence faite à Seignelay (Yonne). 1883.

Rousselot, Paul. *Histoire de l'éducation des femmes en France.* Paris: 1883.

Rulon and Friot. *Un Siècle de pédagogie dans les écoles primaires, 1820-1940.* Paris: 1962.

Sandre, Yves. *Marchands de participes.* Paris: 1962.

Saunders, Mme. J. *Direction maternelle de la jeune fille.* Paris: 1844.

—— *Bonheur ou malheur dans le mariage.* Paris: 1846.

Sauvestre, Charles. *Les Congrégations religieuses.* Enquête: 1867.

Sebillot, P. *Coûtumes populaires de la Haute Bretagne.* Paris: 1886.

Simon, Jules. "L'Instruction primaire et les bibliothèques populaires en France." *Revue des Deux Mondes.* Aug. 15, 1863.

—— "L'Enseignement primaire et les bibliothèques populaires en France." *Revue des Deux Mondes.* Aug. 15, 1864.

—— *L'Ecole.* Paris: 1865, 1894.

—— *Le Gouvernement de M. Thiers.* Paris: 1878, 1879.

—— *L'Instruction gratuite et obligatoire.* Paris: 1873.

—— *La Réforme de l'enseignement secondaire.* Paris: 1876.

Snyders, Georges. *La Pédagogie en France aux XVIIe et XVIIIe siècles.* Paris: P.U.F., 1965.

Taillandier, Saint René. "Les Réformes de l'enseignement primaire." *Revue des Deux Mondes.* June 1, 1870.

Thabault, Roger. *Education and Change in a Village Community, Mazières-en-Gatine, 1848–1914.* New York: 1971.

Théry, Augustin. *Premiers conseils aux mères sur les moyens de diriger et d'instruire leurs filles.* Paris: 1840.

Vaucelles, Louis de. "La Querelle scolaire sous la seconde république à la Guillotière." *Cahiers d'Histoire* 10(1965): 365–388.

Weil, G. *Histoire de l'idée laïque en France au 19e siècle.* Paris: 1925.

—— "Les Républicains et l'enseignement sous Louis Philippe." *Revue Internationale de l'Enseignement.* Janvier, 1899.

Zeldin, T. ed. *Conflicts in French Society, Anticlericalism, Education and Morals in the 19th century.* London: 1970.

Zind, Pierre. *L'Enseignement religieux dans l'instruction primaire publique en France de 1850–1873.* Lyon, 1971.

Index